I AM A MODEL

PROFESSIONAL CAREER GUIDE

BY CAROLYN WALDBUESER

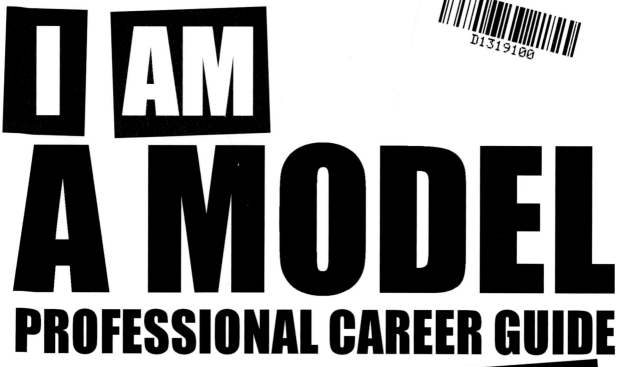

Illustrated and Designed By:
April Waldbueser

Published By
MODEL SHOP COMPANY

TABLE OF CONTENTS

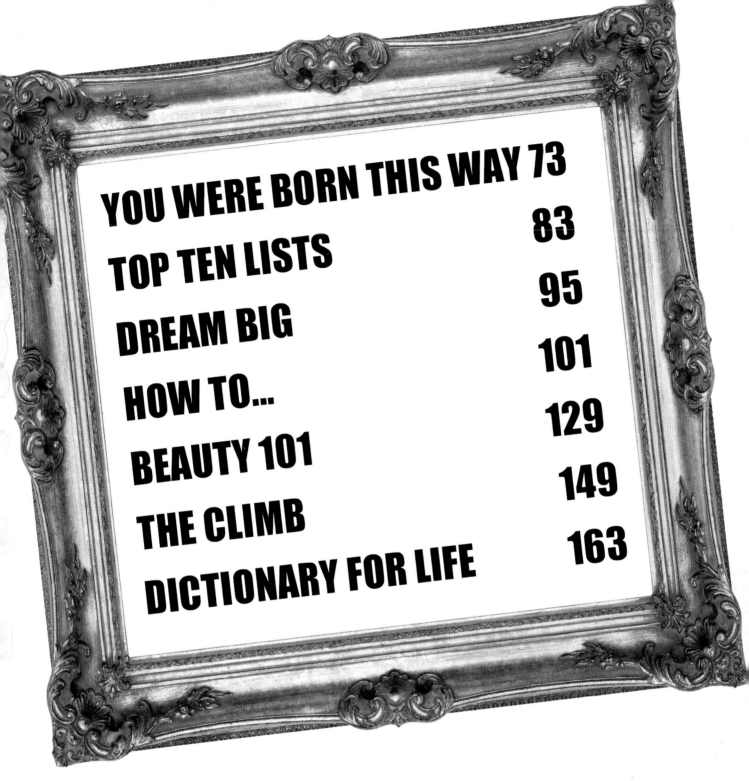

TABLE OF CONTENTS

ABOUT THE

Carolyn Waldbueser

has been a "model maker" for over 30 years. She is the Director of The Miami Fashion Board, placing models with top agencies world wide casting jobs in runway, print-work, tv and film. Carolyn owns Catwalk Productions, the nation's largest network of runway stage events.

For over 3 decades, her team has produced Fashion Shows, Bridal Fairs, and Promotional Conventions from New York to Los Angeles. Her Fashion Show Tour has been in over 350 malls nationwide. In her new book, Carolyn shares the lessons that she has learned, and the wisdom that she has gathered through the years guiding new models into exciting careers in the film and fashion industry.

Carolyn has discovered models who have appeared on the covers of **VOGUE, GLAMOUR, MARIE CLAIRE & SHAPE**
She has found new faces who have appeared in ads for top clients such as:

Calvin Klein, Target, Estee Lauder, Kohl's, JC Penney, Hollister, Claire's & Macy's.

Born in 1954 in Springvale, Georgia, Carolyn is a Cum Laude graduate of the University of Georgia where she studied nutrition and education. Her Model Maker Workshops have helped thousands of people learn the secrets of success and achieve goals beyond their wildest dreams.

Carolyn and her husband Bill have been married for 35 years. Their proudest achievement is their 5 children and 7 grandchildren who are the 2nd and 3rd generation of their family business.

"Success is a series of small disciplines that lead to habits that produce positive results."

— Carolyn Waldbueser

AUTHOR

Join Carolyn and her team on...

THE MIAMI FASHION BOARD CRUISE,

sailing from world famous Miami Beach to the beautiful Bahamas. Book your vacation to paradise NOW and attend one of the most prestigious modeling seminars in the world.

- 3 DAYS AND 3 NIGHTS ABOARD
ROYAL CARIBBEAN
FEATURING:

- PROFESSIONAL MODELING WORKSHOPS

- SIGHTSEEING IN THE BAHAMAS

- PRIVATE ISLAND PICNIC EXCURSION

- SHOWS AND ENTERTAINMENT

Meet The Miami Fashion Board's top bookers and agents. Learn how to develop poise and self confidence on stage and in front of the camera. Cruise the Caribbean with Carolyn and discover how to become a MODEL AND A ROLE MODEL in the film and fashion industry. Bring your book and receive a free Miami Fashion Board T-Shirt. Students will also receive an achievement diploma for professional resumes by completing the model's workshops.

For more information on how to be put on the waiting list to attend, contact our team at: carolyn@catwalkstageproductions.com

PROFESSIONAL
A Note from the Author

This book is a collection of basic knowledge that every working model should know. Whether on a photo shoot or a movie set, there is a professional language that is spoken that everyone who is trained in the industry understands. Just like medical field workers must know the names of drugs and medicine, models must understand the vocabulary of fashion merchandising. In the same way that the medical workers understand how a defibrillator works, likewise, models in the fashion industry should know how to work textures and design while walking on the runway.

Most careers require a college degree with years of studying the craft and perfecting the skills. Models are not required to have a degree, however, they do not just walk off the street and onto the runway. So how does a model earn the respect as a business professional?

A professional model is not just a pretty face. Models are professional employees that understand fashion design and fashion merchandising. Models are not shallow air heads. Models have a basic understanding of business, marketing, advertising, and public relations. Models know how to read a script to make someone laugh or cry. Models know how to captivate an audience by just walking into the room. Although they make it look easy, it is not. Models know how to pose in a swimsuit for a summer catalog in January, when it is 30 degrees on the location set. Models know how to pose in heavy coats for a winter catalog in August, when it is 95 degrees outside on location.

Models study, research, and train in the same way that nurses study, teachers research, and policemen train. A professional model is not someone who happens to be attractive, but rather is someone who knows what they are doing, selling products, merchandise, and

MODELING

fashion in the multi media of runway, print work, television, and film. We all respect trained professionals such as paramedics, firemen, chefs, and secretaries. Now it is time for everyone to understand what it means to work as a professional in the competitive film and fashion industry.

NOW IT IS TIME TO STAND BACK AND WATCH OUT, BECAUSE, "I AM A MODEL!"

This book was written for this purpose. May you read it with delight and study it with joy. May you feel pride and self confidence from the knowledge that you gain.

May this book be the first step on your journey to discovering yourself!

My wish is that this book will inspire you to dream. My hope is that this book will motivate you to get up and follow your dream. And finally my prayer is that you will have the courage to be vulnerable enough to share your talent and gifts with the world. If you do, remember that rejection is a big part of the journey. Criticism goes along with the territory. There will be many failures and mistakes along the way. Success does not happen overnight. Persevere. Hang in there... Enjoy your labor, for it is a gift from God.

"Out of clutter.... Find simplicity. From discord... Find harmony. In the middle of difficulty... Lies opportunity."

-Albert Einstein

MODEL'S FILM AND FASHION IQ TEST

Take the test before you read the book to see what you already know. Take it again after you finish reading the book to discover how much you learned. Just like college textbooks, some of the content needs to be studied, not just read. Some of the content needs to be memorized. Remember, even though you grade yourself here... the real test is when you are on the job. **What will you say when you meet the editor of a magazine? Will you know the difference between commercial and editorial print?** What will you do when you are hired by a fashion photographer for a catalog layout? **Do you just stand there?** What is **SAG and AFTRA? Do you feel like you are on another planet? Well you are! It's called PLANET HOLLYWOOD!** All of the answers to these questions are found in the pages of this book. **Cozy up on a couch with a warm latte & let's go to**

"model's college."

1. Name 2 of the unions governing the film and fashion industry?

    _____

    _____

2. Where is the largest fashion week in the world held?

    _____

3. What is the difference between fashion design and fashion merchandising?

    _____

    _____

    _____

4. What can substitute for a model's dress shield?

    _____

5. Name 4 top agencies:

    _____   _____

    _____   _____

6. What is the difference between a free lance and an exclusive contract?

    _____

    _____

    _____

7. What is a model GO SEE?

    _____

    _____

    _____

8. Name the one of the largest casting boards in America?

9. What fashion magazine hired the very 1st model?

    _____

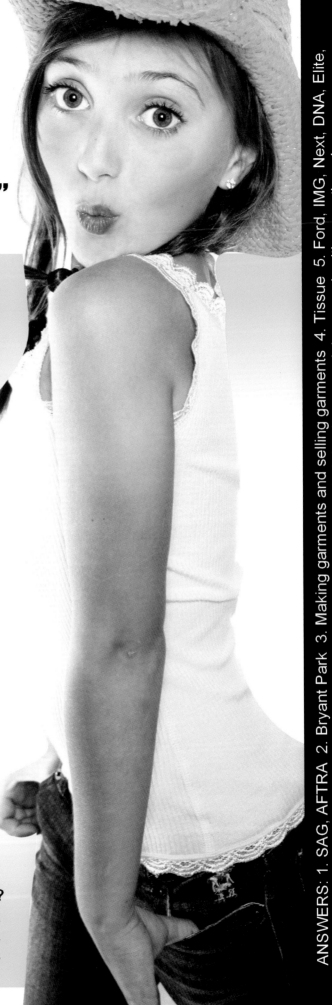

> # "Take the first step in faith.
> ## You don't have to see the whole staircase...
> ## Just take the first step."
> ### -Martin Luther King

10. What is the difference between a feature film and an industrial film?

_____

_____

_____

11. Name 2 ways that a model can work the runway to sell the clothes.

_____

_____

12. List 3 popular design lines of a garment:

_____

_____

_____

13. Name 5 of the top 10 designers:

_____

_____

_____

_____

_____

14. Who is responsible for selecting and choosing the talent for a film project?

_____

15. What does "wrap" mean?

_____

16. What makes a model photogenic?

_____

_____

_____

ANSWERS: 1. SAG, AFTRA 2. Bryant Park 3. Making garments and selling garments 4. Tissue 5. Ford, IMG, Next, DNA, Elite, Wilhelmina, Women, Marilyn, Supreme, NY Models, ONE, Trump 6. A freelance model can work with more than 1 agency. 7. Another word for casting or audition 8. Model Pipeline 9. Vogue 10. Industrial is an instructional video for a company. 11. Feet to the beat, and Facial Expressions 12 Aline, Turtleneck, V-neck, Bell bottom, Hooded, Straight Leg 13. Calvin Klein, Armani, Yves Saint Lauren, Valentino, Coco Chanel, Versace, Halston, Ralph Lauren, Dior, Marc Jacobs 14. Casting Director 15. Filming completed 16. Confidence in front of the camera

IQ TEST
(Continued)

17. What size is a "plus" model?
_____

18. List 3 types of "parts" modeling.
_____
_____
_____

19. List the pay scale ladder of a movie cast.
_____
_____
_____
_____
_____

20. Another name for a "side" is a:
_____

21. Who is Bruce Webber?
_____
_____

22. Name 2 examples of a fabrics texture.
_____
_____

"My philosophy is this: You are responsible for your life and that responsibility begins with **do**ing **your best** at whatever you are doing at this moment."

- Oprah Winfrey

23. List 3 types of fabrics:

_____
_____
_____

24. Name 3 top divas who have had a major impact on the fashion culture`.

_____
_____
_____

25. What is "method" acting?

_____
_____

26. An _____ takes the place of a another performer.

27. What is the job of the executive producer?

_____
_____

28. What is the difference between a monologue & a dialog?

_____
_____
_____

29. A _____ is the fee paid to a model or an actor for the re-use or rebroadcast of their work.

30. Name two "unnatural" foods:

_____
_____

31. A model's invoice to be turned into the agency for a job finished is called a

_____

32. What are the model's 2 missions on the runway?

_____
_____

33. Name 2 mistakes that can cause a model to lose an audition:

_____
_____

34. What does "off book" mean?

_____
_____

35. List 3 items that a model must bring to every audition.

_____
_____
_____

ANSWERS: 17. 12+ 18. Hands, Feet, Legs 19. Extra, Featured, Speaking, Supporting, Starring 20. Script 21. #1 Photographer 22. Stretch, and Pre-washed 23. Satin, Silk, Cotton 24. Marylin Monroe, Lady Gaga, Princess Diana, Jackie Kennedy, Mary Tyler Moore 25. Drawing from past experiences 26. Understudy 27. Financing the Film 28. Monologue is solo 29. Residual 30. French Fries, Jello 31. Voucher 32. Sell the clothes, Entertain the audience 33. Chew Gum, Bring siblings 34. Lines are memorized 35. Portfolio, Casting cards, Resume

KNOW *WHO YOU ARE*

This book is a guide to beginning your journey in the film and fashion industry. It is also a resource for navigating your career course. Most of all, this book is a map to show you the path to "discover yourself!" Finding your true calling in life is to find your true destiny here on Earth. Discovering your true talent is the adventure of a lifetime. This book will be your own personal treasure map as you begin your adventure. But like all maps, it is useless until you know where you are NOW and where you want to go. Once the journey is planned, the map then serves its purpose to "connect the dots," connecting where you are now with where you want to end up. The following people have followed their map successfully. They knew who they were and where they were going. Do you know who you are? Do you know where you are going?

"I AM not afraid. I was born to do this." - Joan of Arc

"I AM awake." - Buddha

"I AM prepared to die, but there is no cause for which I AM prepared to kill." - Gandhi

"I AM a firm believer in the people." - Abraham Lincoln

"I AM the way, the truth, and the life." - Jesus Of Nazareth

"I AM my own experiment. I AM my own work of art." - Madonna

"I AM the toughest golfer mentally in the world." - Tiger Woods

"I AM an artist that draws freely upon my imagination." - Albert Einstein

"I AM always trying that which I cannot do." - Pablo Picasso

"I AM a pencil in the hand of a God who is sending a love letter to the world." - Mother Teresa

"I AM where I AM because I believe in all possibilities." - Whoopi Goldberg

"I AM who I AM and say what I think." - Eminem

"I AM the greatest... I said that even before I knew I was." - Muhammad Ali

"I AM." - God

I AM A MODEL..
ARE YOU?

JOB OPPORTUNITIES
IN THE
FILM & FASHION
INDUSTRY

The industry is bigger than you think. It is filled with talented, beautiful people who make a living working behind the camera's spotlight. The industry is filled with hundreds of job opportunities, from makeup artists to movie directors... from set designers to sound effect technicians... from stand-ins to stunt men; there are countless opportunities. Besides the behind the scenes jobs, below is a list of the different genres that are in front of the camera.

Runway Model
Hair Shows
Pilot Season
Bridal Fairs
Spokesmodels
Foreign Films
Film Actors
Commercial Print
Movie Extras
Radio Voiceovers
TV Commercials
Industrials
Editorial Printwork
Catalog Models
Trade Shows
Promotional Models
Broadcast Journalism
Music Videos
Fashion Print Work
Background Singers
Trunk Shows
Background Dancers

Body "Parts" Models
Overseas Agencies
National Theatre Tours
Singers
Live Mannequins
Independent Film
Theme Parks
Event Host
Broadway Plays

"I've always seen modeling as a stepping stone."

-Tyra Banks

DECLARE YOUR VISION

ONE WORD TO DESCRIBE ME WOULD BE: _____

I WANT TO BE A MODEL BECAUSE: _____
_____
_____

MY BEST PHYSICAL FEATURE IS: _____

MY WORST PHYSICAL FEATURE IS: _____

FIVE YEARS FROM NOW I SEE MYSELF: _____
_____

MY TALENT IS: _____
_____

MY DREAM IS: _____
_____

On one hand, this book can be a shallow superficial picture book for new models to learn fashion and beauty tips, from make-up to weight control. However, on the other hand, if you actually read the text and not just look at the pictures, there is hopefully a great lesson for success hidden between the pages that would be "self help" reading for anyone. "I AM" is not just about being a model. The book could have been titled "I AM a Doctor" with different pictures. The words I Am were first used in the ancient scriptures of Judaism and Christianity. Besides being the name of God, as told to Moses in the great Exodus, I AM also implied that we all are here to discover who "I AM" as we go through life. Our job is a big part of who we become. As children, we all dreamed of growing up "to be" anything from ballerinas or lawyers. Our labor defines our abilities. I AM an artist... I AM a salesman... I AM a teacher... When you finally say I AM a _____ with confidence, you will begin the journey of discovering your destiny. Do you think Steve Jobs was bored at his "job?" I seriously doubt he ever worked a 40 hour week. His destiny was the iPad! His passion was Pixar! He dreamed of itunes and iPhones.

Never settle for a boring dull career punching a timeclock. Living for the weekend to escape your work is the epitomy of a wasted life. Don't just work 9 to 5. Never adopt the mindset of TGIF. Rather find your true vocation where you can truly say "Thank God, it's Monday." You have to have a clear vision. You have to have a goal or a dream. If...

YOU CAN CONCEIVE IT...

YOU CAN BELIEVE IT...

YOU CAN ACHIEVE IT!

"Dream on...
dream until your
dreams,,
come true.
-Aerosmith

Life is but a

"**I dream for a living.**"

-Steven Spielberg

One of my favorite songs of all time is a simple little song called "Row Your Boat." I know that it never reached the Top Forty on the pop charts... And it's not exactly a Rock 'N Roll classic... However, the lyrics of that song should be the philosophy of a model's life. In case you've never heard the little tune, it goes something like this:

"Row, Row, Row Your Boat Gently Down The Stream Merrily, Merrily, Merrily, Merrily Life Is But A Dream"

OK, it's not Beethoven or Mozart. It's certainly not a Beatle's classic... but wait a minute... Could that have been what Paul McCartney meant when he was inspired to write:

DREAM!

"The future belongs to those who believe in the beauty of their dreams."

-Eleanor Roosevelt

"When I Find Myself In Times Of Trouble Mother Mary Comes To Me Speaking Words Of Wisdom Let It Be... Let It Be"

Or maybe "Row Your Boat" inspired Sting to write the haunting lyrics:

"My Soul Is In A Cage. Swim To The Light. Swim To The Light."

If you listen carefully to the message behind a lot of great music, the message is the same. There is " A Bridge Over Troubled Water. "... There is " Amazing Grace. " You see the same message in great art work. The reason The Mona Lisa by Da Vinci became so famous was that she dared to SMILE in such a dark age of a troubled world. What secret did the "Mona Lisa" and the author of "Row Your Boat" know? Is there a lost lesson that our fast paced culture has overlooked? Could this subliminal message actually help you be more successful at your job

and in your relationships? Well, let's examine each line of that song and see if it can apply to your family, your health, your finances, and most importantly your own personal smile.

First... "Row Row Row," life is labor. No one is born to sit on a mountain and meditate. To create, to produce, and to work is an instinct. Watch the world around you. Notice how the ants toil to carry loads... How the squirrels run to and fro storing nuts for the winter... And how the bees buzz from flower to flower working for a living. So what's the point... Whistle while you work! Row... Row... Row...

Next... "Gently Down The Stream." OK, so you are not a salmon. Quit trying to swim upstream. Go with the flow. Life should not be a struggle. Some have made this life way too hard. Some have turned their dream into a nightmare! People who battle food and suffer through diets are usually over weight. Tight wads, misers, and stingy people usually end up broke. People who struggle to be holy and religious on the outside usually are not very spiritual on the inside. I could struggle every day training to be a doctor but I don't like blood. I could strain and strain to be a musician, but it's just not me. I could try my hardest to be a pilot, but I don't enjoy flying. Catwalk Productions is my perfect platform to utilize all of my strengths and my talents. I could never do anything else. I love it. It's who I am. I work hard, but I smile everyday. It's not forced or fake. It's my natural personality to be at a stage. It is my gift to encourage people to stand on a stage and shine. It is my destiny to succeed at what I enjoy doing. Some of you have lost your SMILE. The world is not against you. There is no such thing as bad luck. Get over yourself. Never waste time doubting your ability or stressing over your circumstances.

Any model's career is like a giant powerful locomotive that is leaving the station with a proven track record for success. New rookie models then hop on board and stand behind their seats inside the train pushing forward with all of their might struggling and sweating profusely to help the train reach its destination. Sit down in your train seat and enjoy the ride. Let your passion carry you to where you want to go. RELAX!! Guess what? You don't have to strain to have a successful audition. Losing an audition is not the end of the world. Blaming and complaining is a downward spiral that only goes in circles and leads to nowhere.

If you cannot smile as you walk away from an audition, win or lose, you should strongly consider finding labor that you do enjoy somewhere else. In other words, don't ever blame anyone else for your unhappiness. Don't journey through four or five jobs and two or three marriages looking for happiness. You will never find peace or contentment in any outside source. It's not there. Modeling alone can never satisfy you. Your family can not jump through hoops to keep you entertained. So what is the answer? What is the secret? How do we find true success? Men have searched for centuries in vain attempts to find real happiness and failed. Even Indiana Jones chased clues around the world for 4 movies and never quite found success... So what do the Mona Lisa and I both have in common? We both know why we are smiling! Why? Because

Successful people focus on their goal... Unsuccessful people focus on the obstacles in front of their goal. Successful people are proactive. Unsuccessful people are reactive. Successful people take full responsibility. Unsuccessful people blame others and make excuses.

the Ark of the Covenant is not hidden under a stone or buried in a deep cave. It is inside of us.

"To believe in the things that you can see and touch is no belief at all... but to believe in the unseen... is both a triumph and a blessing."

- Abraham Lincoln

In the Wizard of Oz, Dorothy could never find the answer in the Emerald City. So what was it? What did she discover in the end? The Wizard certainly did not have it. The answer to her destiny was in her heart all along. She alone had the power to regain her lost happiness. Like Indiana Jones and Dorothy, the SMILE has been inside of you the whole time and you didn't know it was there. Your dormant volcano of power has been waiting to erupt and explode over your circumstances. The power does not come from modeling. Success has nothing to do with winning or landing a

job. *Real* happiness comes from knowing that deep inside of you there is a light. Below the surface of your personality, there is a connection that you feel to a source that is stronger than you!

It's difficult to feel the connection in a crowd or above the noise. The next time you are alone, listen to your heart. The next time you are afraid, be still, be silent, and wait for it... **Life is but a dream!**

I have learned to forgive when being slandered. I have learned to breathe when being sued. I have genuinely learned how to love my enemies. I have learned from. Martin Luther King that nonreaction and nonviolence can create a revolution. I have learned from Gandhi, that if you want to change the world, you must BE the change that you desire. And we all learned from Micheal Jackson, "I'm starting with the man in the mirror, asking him to change his ways. No message could've been any clearer. If you wanna make the world a better place. Take a look at yourself, and make a change."

"If you really want something... you can figure out how to make it happen."

-Cher

Question? Why do some people succeed and soar to great heights.... while other people, doing the same thing, fail miserably?

Answer! The people succeeding are "causing" their own success. The people failing are the "effect" of their own failure.

FIND YOUR PASSION
DISCOVER YOUR DREAM!

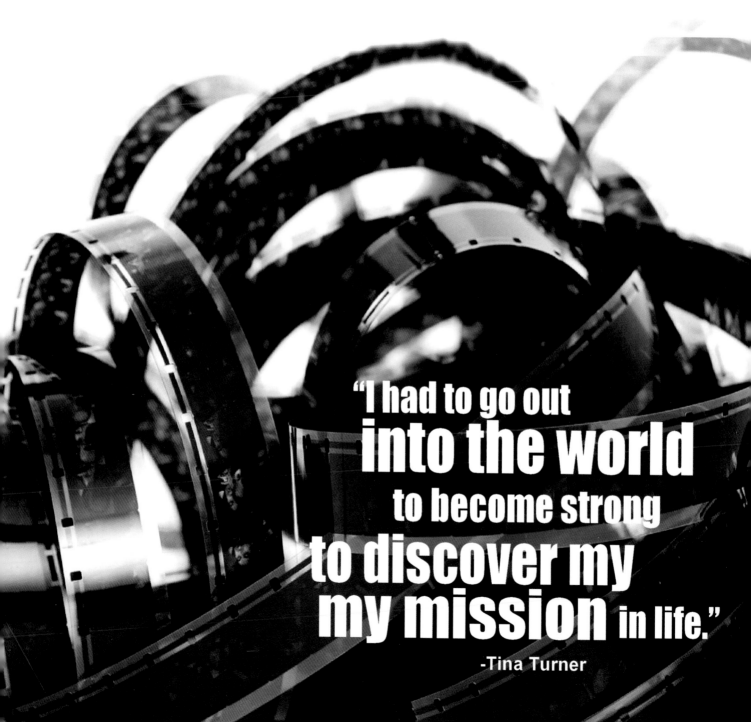

"I had to go out **into the world** to become strong **to discover my my mission** in life."

-Tina Turner

MATCH THE "DESIRE" WITH THE "DO"

DESIRE	DO
I LOVE TO TRAVEL	BECOME A MISSIONARY
I LOVE TO DRAW	BECOME AN AUTHOR
I LOVE TO ACT	BECOME A PRO ATHLETE
I LOVE TO BUILD THINGS	BECOME A MUSICIAN
I LOVE TO CARE FOR PEOPLE	BECOME AN ACTOR
I LOVE TO WRITE	BECOME A PILOT
I LOVE TO ENTERTAIN	BECOME A SONGWRITER
I LOVE TO WRITE POETRY	BECOME AN ENTREPRENEUR
I LOVE TO CREATE	BECOME AN ARCHEOLOGIST
I LOVE TO PLAY THE GUITAR	BECOME AN ARTIST
I LOVE TO EXPLORE	BECOME AN ARCHITECT
I LOVE TO PLAY SPORTS	BECOME A DOCTOR
I LOVE TO HELP PEOPLE	BECOME A MODEL
I LOVE TO SELL STUFF	BECOME AN INVENTOR

"I stand for freedom of expression, doing what you believe in, and going after your dreams."

— Madonna

Discover

"In order to be irreplaceable, you must

I am, obviously, an author. Sometimes, I wake up at 4:30 in the morning... just to write! Isn't that crazy? Well it is, if you don't have the "talent" to put thoughts into words on paper. Some people get up before dawn to work out because they have a passion to be a pro athlete. Parents should take clues from a child's natural personality when steering them into extra curricular activities. Don't force a kid to take piano lessons who whines about practicing. You're probably wasting your money on music lessons. On the other hand, if your child just broke your neighbor's window by hitting a baseball over the fence.... You might want to channel that energy and put them in Little League. GO WITH THE FLOW. Don't go against the grain. Talent and abilities should be nurtured and developed. True talent will stand the test of time. I have seen many "want-to-be" stars who declared their passion for the film industry, burn out after one week on a real movie set working 15 hour days. They quickly realized that they actually hated "the craft" of acting when they learned that it was hard work. They really just wanted to be famous. Stars are not discovered! They are talented models who have spent years developing their acting ability. Halle Berry did not win the Academy Award because she has a pretty face! She is the L'oreal model.... Because "she's worth it." Everyone, let me repeat, everyone has a talent. This talent is the source of an ability to do something extremely well. The ability to sing or dance.... or the talent to play a sport or paint a picture are all examples of "God given" gifts. Our talent is usually also our passion. Singers sing in the shower and artists doodle on paper. Real talent cannot be bought through lessons. It cannot be faked or imitated. I could take years of voice lessons and never sing like Mariah Carey. My sons tried for years to "be like Mike" practicing basketball, hoping to be the next Michael Jordan. Unfortunately, they were not born with his gift. Mariah or Michael do not struggle to use their abilities. Rather, there is a natural flow or nonresistance to what they do.

So you think you're cute... Get over yourself. Pretty faces are a dime a dozen. Many parents believe that their "beautiful child" has what it takes to be a model. What a horrible lesson to teach a child that their "looks" are all they need to win. Parents who push children into modeling because they think they are gorgeous, are only setting their kids up for future low self esteem. No one wants to be judged for their looks or compared to other's appearances. Modeling is not a beauty pageant. If you think you are ALL THAT and you believe that your face is your "gift", then go try out to be MISS AMERICA. If you really think that you are "ridiculously good looking," go rent the movie, "Zoolander." **Remember, being pretty is not a talent.**

Yourself!
always be different." -COCO CHANEL

CHAPTER 6

THIS IS HOW WE "ROLE"
ROLE MODELS 101

Beauty really is only skin deep. That is why most models are usually branded as being shallow. If you are serious about working long term in the deep waters of this highly competitive industry, then you must dig deeper than your cute face to find hidden wisdom and dormant talent. These treasures that are buried deep within your personality are waiting to be tapped. You will quickly discover that your real value is not your LOOKS, but your CHARACTER. Your real talents will be revealed to be the foundation of your career. Models come and go very quickly. Role models endure the test of time.

ROLE MODELS

Success is a series of small disciplines that lead to habits that produce positive results. Below are a list of small positive disciplines.

1. Set Goals
2. Create a Healthy Lifestyle
3. Live With Passion
4. Exemplify Integrity
5. Finish What You Start
6. Balance Mind, Body, and Soul
7. Demonstrate Self Control
8. Practice Humility
9. Develop Real Relationships
10. Master Time Management
11. Spend Money Wisely
12. Become Smart, Savvy Professionals

ROLE MODELS

Failure is a series of small disciplines that lead to habits that produce negative results. Below are a list of small negative disciplines.

1. Drink Too Much
2. Spend More Than You Make
3. Throw Temper Tantrums
4. Eat Empty Calories
5. Sleep Around
6. Curse Like A Sailor
7. Do Drugs
8. Party Late and Oversleep
9. Become Spoiled and Arrogant
10. Slip Into Bad Habits
11. Become Shallow Airheads
12. Forget Where You Came From

List two positive habits and negative habits that are leading you towards success or towards failure.

_____   _____

_____   _____

DO...

DON'T...

Who's Your Role Model?

Write their name here: _____

S-U-C-C-E-S-S... That's the way you spell "success." When I was a cheerleader in middle school, that was one of my favorite cheers. Unfortunately, success was measured by if we won or lost the football game. Fifty years later, with thousands of life games behind me, no longer do I evaluate success by the score at the end of the game. Players who have the highest score are not necessarily successful. The richest models are not always the happiest. Fame is not an accurate measurement of success. How many athletes, celebrities, and super models do you know who won the Oscar or landed the contract only to end up in rehab or failed relationships? In a world where Charlie Sheen is "winning," it may be difficult to understand what winning really is. And even though Coke is "the real thing," you may want to read the ingredients to search for any ingredients that are really real or natural. Our culture worships rock idols and adores movie stars as role models to imitate.... BUT BE VERY CAREFUL, BEFORE YOU FOLLOW SOMEONE...

Be careful to notice where they are going and how they got there. Don't analyze their bank account to judge their success. Analyze their contentment with themselves.... their purpose in life... their joy... their love... their fruit. Real role models are few and far between. Remember every job, every marriage, everyday life has its challenges and rewards, ups and downs, as well as good and bad days! Real lasting success is sustained not for just weeks, months, years, or decades, but for a LIFETIME. Success does not come from your IQ, but from your CQ. Your Intelligence Quotient can only carry you so far; after that, role models must have a Challenge Quotient! Real role models know how to face challenges every day, big or small, few or many. It took Moses to face the Red Sea and lead the people of Egypt through the water. It took David to face Goliath with courage and bravery, when no one else would face the giant, and it took Joshua to lead the charge against the Wall of Jericho when things looked hopeless.

My husband, Bill, is my role model. He's not famous. No one has ever asked for his autograph. He doesn't have Brad Pitt's

"The fight is won or lost far away from witnesses. It is won in the gym long before I dance under the lights."
- Muhammad Ali

hair... He's BALD! He doesn't have a cover model's face. He's a little "quirky" as they say, if he would go to a casting. His physique after 60 years is no longer buffed, and his abs disappeared somewhere in his forties. So why do I still think that he is the most beautiful man on Earth?

I have watched him for almost four decades face unbelievable challenges. I've watched as he never looked down in the face of many giants and obstacles that were in our path. He has faced challenges, enemies, and problems without hesitation. He has been knocked down, but never knocked out. He does not run from challenges. He does not quit when things get hard or difficult. Quitting leads you in a circle. If you quit and run, you will eventually spiral in the same circular patterns. Eventually, everyone must face their giant. Bill has taught me by example to face my fears and standup to my enemy! I have watched Bill stay on a straight path, never turning back or running in a circle looking for

something easier. Why? Because, of his commitment to being a success as a young boy. He has run his race and reached his goals. Make it a goal to: Build your Career, Build your Family, and most of all Build your Dream!

Success in any field begins as a "mental game". It's all in your mind! Whether you are on a golf course, a tennis court, or a basketball court, your ability to win begins by your mental attitude towards winning. How much time do you use your mind each day to think about winning or being successful at work? How much time each day do your allow your mind to waste time worrying, struggling, complaining, blaming, fretting and fuming about your job? Negative thoughts create negative energy, that create negative results. Most importantly, you create a negative person. A negative person is usually filled with anger or fear. That kind of person does not only NOT attract

clients, but they are usually hard to get along with and difficult to live with. Negative energy effects your health, strength, emotions, relationships, and of course, your castings and auditions. So begin today. Start being aware of your thoughts, your emotions, and your mental attitude everyday. Be honest with yourself. Are you addicted to negativity? Are you a chronic worrier and constant complainer? Do you know someone who is? Do you work or live with someone who is? First, understand that negative energy drains the body of its life force. Negative people are usually depressed, lethargic, sickly, and run down in general poor health. They usually try to regain energy by stealing other people's energy, kind of like an "energy vampire." They argue, scream, belittle, blame, complain, and yell at all the people around them, trying to regain lost energy.

"Character cannot be developed in ease and calm... only by experience and trials can the soul be strengthened... ambition inspired and success achieved."

- Helen Keller

Real success`, physically, emotionally, socially, mentally, romantically, spiritually, and financially, will be a feeling of wellness, a deep contentment of who you are, and a sense of peace that everything is OK. No matter what the final score!

"We are taught you can blame your father, your sister, your brother, your teachers, anyone but yourself. It's never your fault... but actually it's always your fault! If you want to change, you are the only one with the power to change. It's that simple."

- Katherine Hepburn

Chapter 10

THE INDUSTRY

A TO Z

"Logic will take you from A-Z. IMAGINATION will take you everywhere."

- Albert Einstein

The following chapter is a model's dictionary.

These definitions must be studied & memorized.

NOTHING is more embarrassing, than to be paid as a professional model, only to be exposed as knowing NOTHING about your trade and craft!

Also, NOTHING will give you more self confidence on a professional set, than to know your stuff.

Do you want to be respected & admired as a professional model? OK, let's do our homework.

Actor:

An employee who performs a role as a character in a story.

A.F.T.R.A.:

The union "American Federation Of Television and Radio Artists"

Agency:

An office that employs models for casting in the Film and Fashion Industry.

Agent Commission:

The money taken from a model's gross check to pay the agent's salary for managing the model's career... Usually 10%-20%.

Accessory:

An additional item added to an outfit to enhance the style of the garment such as... belts, jewelry, scarves, hats, jackets or purses.

Audition:

A tryout for a film or fashion role, usually in front of a casting director.

"Our doubts are traitors that will cause us not to win."
-William Shakespeare

Booker:

The employer at an agency responsible for matching job opportunities with the right model to fill the job.

Bridal Show:

A fashion show highlighting the latest fashions and trends for the wedding party.

Broadway

A street in NYC that is the world's "Mecca" of stage productions.

Bruce Webber

One of the top fashion photographers in the world.

Bryant Park:

The venue in NYC where the famous world renown Fashion Week is held.

"I'm laughing because I know the **secret of life.** The secret is that I know that I am worth more than **my house** or my bank account."

- Carlos Santana

Clapper Board: The board that a
director's assistant uses to document the scene's date, time, and location in front of the camera for later editing purposes.

Client: A business or company that
hires an agency to provide a model or an actor.

Complexion: The quality of a model's
skin. Skin should be clean and clear because camera close-ups reveal blemishes, dark circles, and oily skin.

Child Labor Laws:
Laws passed to protect minors under 19 years of age, from unfair or unhealthy working environments.

Community Theater:
A group of amateur performers who produce a play in a local theater solely for the enjoyment of the craft of acting. A great place for young model and actors, singers and dancers to develop new skills in front of an audience.

CFDA: Council of Fashion Design of America.

Diane von Fürstenberg has been the president since 2006.

Call Back: A request that a model come back for an additional screening.

Campaign: A multi media advertising extravaganza that launches a new product or line.

Casting Board: An internet website listing auditions and castings in the film and fashion industry.

Casting Cards: An identification card for models used at auditions. This card is different than a business card, as it showcases the model's look with one or more photos.

Collection: A designer's montage of selections for the new fashion season. "Vera Wang Spring Collection."

Costume Jewelry: A model's, favorite accessory! Earrings, Necklaces, Rings, and Bracelets.

"The mind is an enemy to those who do not control it."

-The Bhagarad Gita

Diet: A model's diet should consist of mostly natural water based foods such as fruits and vegetables that provide daily protein and vitamin requirements. Carbohydrates should be enjoyed with limitations.... junk foods, that are empty calories, should be enjoyed as occasional treats.

Diva: A trendy term to describe a model or actor with a reputation for being difficult or spoiled.

Demo Reel: A video tape showcasing a performer's talents or skills.

Digital Portfolio: A collection of the model's best work on camera that can be electronically shown to clients for castings.

Dress Shields: A small pad purchased at a drug store worn under the model's armpits to protect the clothing from perspiration stains. Tissue may be used when professional pads are unavailable.

Designer: A professional garment maker who creates unique styles for the fashion industry.

Editorial Model:

A model hired for the pages of a magazine that tells a story or creates an emotion from photos. (The pages that ARE NOT paid advertisements.)

Exclusive Contract:

A model's agreement to work exclusively for one agency.

Fashion Design:

A 4-Year college degree to learn the art of creating fashion... similar to architectural or interior design.

Fashion Merchandising:

A college degree to learn the technique of marketing, buying and selling garments in the fashion industry... similar to a business or advertising degree.

Fabric: The raw material used to make clothes such as wool, silk, cotton, or denim.

Fashion Show: An event where models walk on a runway, posing and moving to enhance the fit of the garment and the feel of the fabric.

Fashion Week: A week designated in the Spring and again in the Fall to introduce designers' new styles and launch new collections for the upcoming season.

Fashionista: Someone who " shops till they drop" or hunts for bargains. Obsesses with fashion. Shopaholic.

Free lance: A model who is not represented by an agency. A model who manages their own career.

Figure: A model's figure should have proportionate measurements. The breast and the hips should match numbers... with the waistline being 10 inches less. Examples: (34-24-34) (38-28-38) (40-30-40)

G

Grip:

The person hired to set up the lighting on a film project.

Go See:

An appointment for a model to "Go-See" a client for a potential booking.

Haute Couture:

A french term that translates "high sewing"... Refers to the creation of custom-made hand crafted garments.

Height:

In the past, editorial models for high fashion were usually 5'7" and taller. However, today's trends are eliminating height and size requirements altogether. Queen Latifah and Ellen Degeneres as models for COVER GIRL MAKEUP are examples.

Headshot:

A close-up photo of a model or actor's face for identification at a casting or audition.

Industrial: A film about a company's product or service used as a commercial for sale purposes and not for entertainment.

Invoice: A record of a model's time on the job for payment or salary.

Independent Film: A feature movie produced by a company that is not a major motion picture studio. Small, independent film makers hire models and actors with small resume`s, due to their limited budgets. They provide great launching pads for new careers.

Icon: Someone who has risen to the top of their field and is admired and respected. Audrey Hepburn, Barbra Streisand, and Denzel Washington are icons that have stood the test of time.

It Girl: The girl of the hour! The next big thing! The one to watch!

"Don't miss the **opportunity** to become **who you want to be.**"
-Jon Bon Jovi

Job:

Modeling is a job. It is not a "get rich quick" climb to fame and fortune. Very few models become celebrities and most models are not super wealthy. Models are employees in the film and fashion industry who work for a living.

Kitsch:

A style incorporating elements from popular culture.

"Being **fearless** is living in spite of the things that **scare** you to death."

- Taylor Swift

Ladder: Promotional scale for a film project.
- Extra   - Featured Extra   -Principal Role
- Supporting Role   - Co-starring Role   -Starring Role

Location Shoot: A photo shoot
not shot in a photographer's studio, but shot on location at a beach, on the street, or whatever backdrop enhances the style or mood of the photograph.

"Look": A model who possesses all of the
qualities and features of the popular trends of the season.

Line: The shape and silhouette of a garment.
- Turtle neck sweater   - Hooded Jacket   - Aline Skirt
- Bell bottom pants   - Straight leg jeans   - V-Neck

Live Mannequin: A human
model hired to portray a mannequin by freeze modeling in a store window display.

Manager: A person who manages a
model's schedule and bookings.

"Expose yourself to your deepest fear, after that, fear has no power. When fear vanishes, you are free."

- Jim Morrison (The Doors)

Makeup: A model's makeup should cover

blemishes, dark circles, and complexion imperfections. Eyes and lips should be lined to enlarge facial features... and darker colors should be used, so not to look washed out under bright, hot lights.

Model Pipeline: The largest

casting board for freelance models to find auditions in the film and fashion industry. www.modelpipeline.com

Model's Bag: Professional models

always bring a large tote to carry essentials for their work; such as casting cards, portfolio, shoes, dress shields, makeup, and hair brush.

Mother Agent: A model's original

scout that discovered them. The person that was essential in their breaking into the industry. Mother agencies are usually paid a "finder fee" or scouting commission.

Make Over: A change of style, hair

or makeup, that improves a models overall look.

"**Our greatest glory**
is not in never falling...
but in getting up
every time you do."
- Confucious

Magazine: A fashion magazine
creates trends and styles that influence the
fashion culture. A model's dream is to land
a job in a top fashion magazine.

Music Video: A model is hired to
enhance the look and feel of a song. Background
dancer or character actor...

Market: An urban area that has many
advertising and promotional companies that hire
models. Such as New York, Paris, and Milan.

Method Acting: Using experiences
from your personal life to help produce a mood or
create an emotion on stage. An example is using a
memory of a personal broken relationship to bring real
emotion to a sad script.

Model: A person hired to promote products
or services.

Monologue: A solo script.

"**Ask** and you will recieve...
Seek and you will find...
Knock and the
door will open."
-Jesus

Nutrition:
A model's complexion, weight, hair and nails are all influenced by the type of foods eaten every day. You are what you eat!

Now:
Living in the moment... Making the best out of today. Not regretting the past or worried about the future. "Life isn't about waiting for the storm to pass. It's about learning to dance in the rain!"

Natural Foods:
Any food that is found in nature such as oranges or avocados. Unnatural foods are not found in nature, and are usually packaged and highly processed. There is no such thing as macaroni plant or a gelatin bush.

Non Exclusive:
A model who is signed to an agency part time; therefore, has the right to work with other agencies, and the right to freelance as well.

Orthodontics:
Straight teeth are a must for camera close ups. Braces, caps, crowns, and veneers offer models a wide variety of options for beautiful smiles.

"Hard work **beats talent...** when talent doesn't **work hard.**"
-Tim Tebow,
Denver Bronco's Quarterback

Off Book: When an actor or spokes model has memorized the lines and no longer needs a script.

Photo-Shoot: A session with a photographer to create a "look."

Portfolio: A collection for photos of a model used as a resume and to show a model's range and versatility.

Print work: Modeling jobs in catalogs, magazines, and newspapers.

Photogenic: A model's ability to be "natural" in front of the camera.

Photoshop: An editor's touch up to improve a photograph.

"There is a great **freedom** when your feet are in two worlds... The world of **flesh** and the world of **Spirit.**"
- Bono

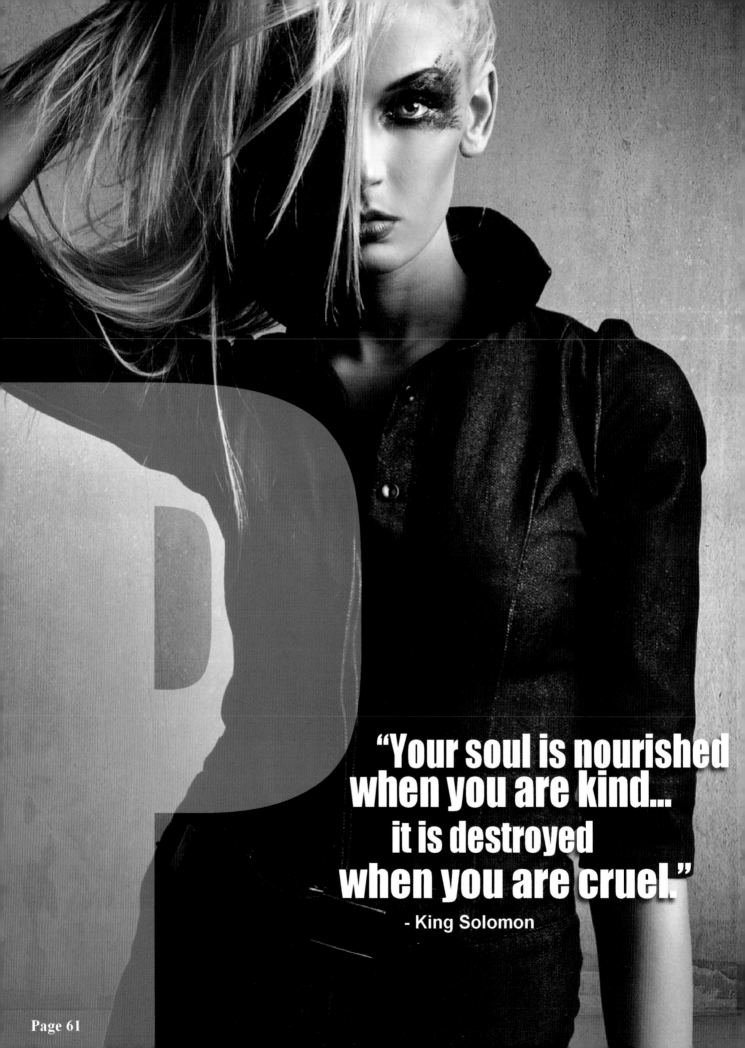

"Your soul is nourished
when you are kind...
it is destroyed
when you are cruel."
- King Solomon

Polyester: A synthetic fabric in contrast
to fabrics from natural sources like wool and cotton.

Pose: A model's use of the human body to
enhance the shape of the garment and the emotion
of the outfit such as: tilt of the neck, facial expression,
extended arms, twist of the torso.

PA: A production assistant on the set of a film shoot.

Plus Model: Any model who is size 12
or larger. Models come in all shapes and sizes.
Catalogs show size 18 as well as size 8. Models
are hired by their ability to be photogenic in front of
the camera and not by their hip size.

Parts: A division for a modeling agency that
specializes in body parts.... For example a hand model
for jewelry or a foot model for shoes.

"Quiet" on the set: Directors
ingo instructing the cast and crew that filming is
about to start.

"**I meditate** and
pray everyday
I am still a work
in progress."
- Halle Berry

Runway model: Walking on a ramp to promote fashions. (See Rock The Runway for tips)

References: Former employers who will provide a recommendation on your behalf.

Rehearsal: "Practice Makes Perfect."
Whether attending a dress rehearsal before a show or memorizing lines in your home, a successful model is diligent in preparing to be polished for perfection. Competition is tough and only the models who do their homework finish first.

Role model: A model who is beautiful inside and out. Someone who is respected and admired by their peers. Someone who sets a high standard and leads by example.

Spokes Model: A job requiring a model to speak such as a TV Commercial or Voiceover.

Scout: An agency employee whose job

is to discover new talent and develop new faces. Many models have been scouted in airports and restaurants. YouTube is the latest platform for launching new careers.

Skincare: Models are required to wear

heavy makeup and work under hot lights, which can be detrimental to their skin. Models should remove all makeup immediately after work. Cleansing and moisturizing are essential to long term beautiful skin.

Screen Test: A video demonstration of

a model's ability to read a script and walk the runway. Clients look for poise and personality, as well as charisma and the X factor.

Super Model: A term made famous

when a group of models became multi-millionaires as "Icons" of a generation. (Example: Cindy Crawford)

Script: Written dialog for a speaking role.

Also known as "sides."

"I am looking for a lot of men who have the infinite capacity to **believe** the **impossible.**"
- Henry Ford

"I always wanted to be something. I guess I should have been more specific.

- Lily Tomlin

Talent: A God given talent or ability to perform such as: Singer, Dancer, or Musician.

Tear sheets: Copies of a model's professional pages from a catalog or magazine added to their portfolio to build their resume`s.

Tattoo: Although popular in today's culture, tattoos are taboo for models. Clients require models to wear a special kind of makeup to cover up tattoos while on the set.

Teleprompter: A machine that feeds the words to the spokesmodel across the bottom of the camera.

Texture: The fit and feel of the fabric. Spandex will stretch. Linen will wrinkle. Burlap is scratchy. Pre-washed denim is soft.

Typecast: A stereotype of a certain look which helps a model land a role. For example: an Asian male might be "typecast" to book a martial artist role.

Union: An organization to legally represent the employees in the film and fashion industry.

Understudy: Someone who is hired as an alternate to the position. The understudy replaces the employee in case of illness or absence.

Un-photogenic: A model who is not natural in front of the camera. A model may be pretty, but stiff on film, thus making them un-photogenic.

Vogue: The first fashion magazine. Vogue of Paris hired the first model to advertise clothing.

Versatility: A model's ability to demonstrate a wide variety of looks and emotions. A model should develop the ability to look older and younger. Displaying different characters in your portfolio is necessary so you aren't typecast in one role type. A good example of versatility is John Travolta. He can play the bad guy in *Swordfish*, the hero in *Saturday Night Fever*, the loving father in *Look Who's Talking*, the singing dancing heart throb in *Grease*, the comedian in *Old Dogs*, the terrorist in *Face Off* and even a woman in *Hairspray*!

"When I was a **child** I was a **dreamer.** Every dream I ever dreamed **has come true.**"

- Elvis Presley

Weight control: A model's figure must represent a body shape that is healthy and fit. All models are not thin, but all models are toned. Exercise is a part of every successful model's daily routine.

Wilhelmina: One of America's first supermodels. After retirement at an early age she started one of the top ten modeling agencies in the world.

X factor: A model or actor's unique ability to stand out at an audition due to his aura of success and magnetism that attracts attention.

YouTube: A popular media for showcasing new faces and undiscovered talent.... Justin Beiber's You tube demo launched him from obscurity to stardom.

Yoga: The exercise increasing a model's muscle tone and flexibility. Yoga also creates a balance of mind, body, and soul.

Zoolander: A popular movie icon stereo typing the vanity of male models.

"**Success**
comes from
within...
not without"
- Ralph Waldo Emerson

Chapter 11

YOU WERE BORN THIS WAY

-Lady Gaga

MASTERMIND
YOUR FATE

The greatest power that we have as human beings is the capacity to choose to express who we are. Every moment of everyday gives us opportunities to use this power in our words and actions while declaring and defining our personality and our character. By simply expressing kindness in a situation, we become a kind person. To demonstrate courage, is to become a brave person. In the same way, an act of dishonesty leads you to become a dishonest person. To blow up in a fit of anger, molds you unconsciously into a mean person. Before there is an action, there is first a thought. For example, before a murderer kills someone, he first must have had thoughts of hatred. Before a thief steals, they entertain thoughts of envy and greed. If OJ Simpson had been trained to discipline his mind with *right* thinking instead of *wrong* thinking, he might still be the football hero that he was to all of us. What caused him to lose his Heisman Trophy? His life was steered in the wrong direction by first entertaining THOUGHTS of anger. His *I AM* a star... changed to *I AM* a prisoner, not by luck or by chance, but by his own power to create who he was. Shakespeare said it best when he wrote his famous script:

"To be... or not to be... That is the question."
-Shakespeare

We all have the power inside of us to create who we will *"be"*, moment by moment... day by day... by thinking... daydreaming... meditating... praying.... who we want to be. Everyone daydreams... meditates... and prays... whether they recognize it or not. The key to your destiny though, is WHAT YOU THINK and meditate about. Have you ever heard someone be reprimanded for a crazy action with *"WHAT WERE YOU THINKING????!"* Obviously they were thinking before they were acting. What most people don't realize is that you automatically become addicted to what you think about. People who meditate and dream about sex, usually become addicted to pornography or abnormal sexual behavior. People who allow themselves to worry, usually become manic depressants or hypochondriacs. On the other hand, individuals who know how to guard their mind and discipline their thought life usually become positive people with successful results. The SECRET to making a thought become reality is repetition of thought. Everyday I am tempted to be mad, angry or hurt. I have learned to recognize thoughts of jealousy, pride and hatred, and I have also learned how to breathe deeply, and erase those negative thoughts from my mind and replace them with healthy, positive thoughts. Five minutes of anger, can seep poisonous toxins into the body. Ulcers, strokes, and high blood pressure are all the results of a stressed body... and a stressed body is the result of stressed thinking. Here are a couple of concrete steps that have helped me.

"You must **never be fearful** about what you are doing, when you know that what you are doing **is right.**"

- Rosa Parks

Step #1 Do not listen to PRAISE OR *criticism*

"I've always taken risks, and never worried what the world might think of me."

- Cher

Praise and criticism are the same thing. They are both measurements of other people's opinion about yourself. Neither one of them matters. Don't listen to praise. It will only puff you up and give you a *"big head."* Criticism, other than sincere constructive criticism, should be shaken off and dismissed. Ridicule and rejection are both forms of unhealthy criticism. From scorned contestants on American Idol, to bullied kids in middle school, everyone at one time or another, has felt the sting of the judgement of other people. However, what most people do not realize is that praise is just as toxic and poisonous as criticism. The more praise a super model gets, the more aloof they become. Celebrities who are constantly stalked by adoring paparazzi, become paranoid people. Isn't it true that the more praise and popularity that a star gets, the more of a recluse they become. Many models and actors lose their identity as they are engulfed in a world of praise from other people. Elvis Presley would come off of a stage where adoring fans were worshiping him, only to run away from all of the praise, to begin his drug induced private world. He would then be given more drugs to wake him up and stimulate him to go out and face the praise of his fans the next night. Sadly, Elvis was a role model for Michael Jackson, who followed his hero down the same path. Praise is just as deadly as criticism. Other people's

Your life is the reflection of who you believe that you are!

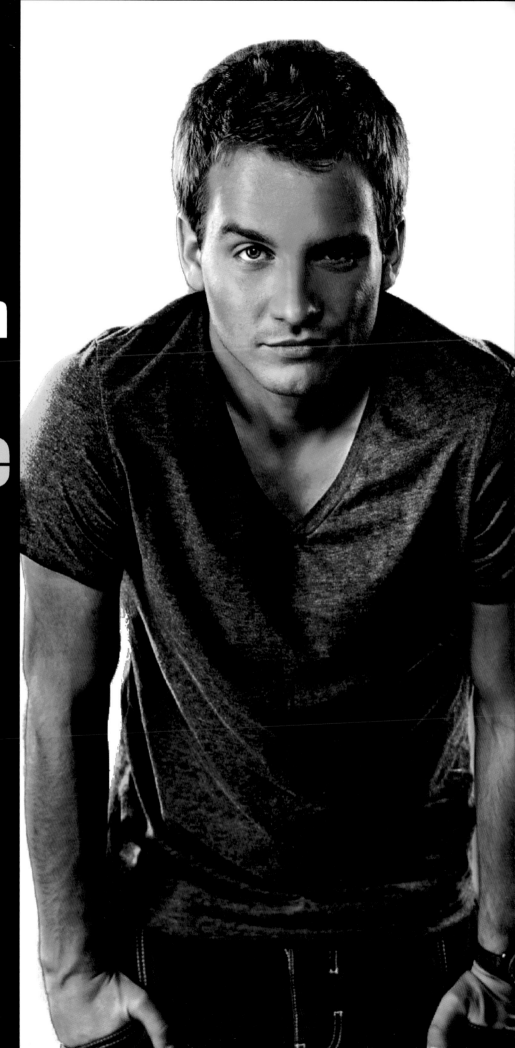

Step #2

You cannot control what happens moment by moment, but you can control how you react to what happens.

For example: let's take 2 people riding a roller coaster. One person thinks *I AM* enjoying this. *I AM* loving this... thereby releasing endorphins into their body, which creates a positive fun experience. Another person sitting next to them, thinks *I AM* not enjoying this. *I AM* afraid... thereby releasing adrenaline into the body which creates a negative, terrifying experience. The roller coaster ride is the same for both people. It is their thinking reaction to the experience that is the difference.

Step #3

Discipline yourself to put action behind every thought

I can say *"I AM"* an athlete every day, but if I do not make myself do something athletic everyday with that thought, I AM only fooling myself. I can say *I AM* thin and healthy everyday, but if I purposely eat ice cream every day, my words are wasted. Faith without *works is dead.*

Your talk must become your walk. Actions always speak louder than words to your subconscious mind. The thought of I AM unsuccessful... is usually followed by actions of sleeping in, and wasting time. The thought of I AM successful... is usually followed by actions of rising early with enthusiasm and excitement for productivity.

Everyday you make powerful creative choices of *"being"*. The reality of what you accomplish in actions is a true testimony to what you are thinking. True peace in your life is when you reach a state of self acceptance and love that is so complete, that you are truly free of anyone's opinion about who you are except for your own. This is why other people's opinions of me do not shape who *I am*. Unfair judgment and criticism from mean and angry people, if not accepted by you, will return to themselves like a boomerang & KARMA is a BITCH! "*Give and it shall be given back to you.*" Can you imagine what some people are getting paid back for what they've *"given"* to you? I know who I AM, regardless of praise or criticism.

Long ago, Bill and I knew if we were going to run a company, that we would have to *be* brave and fearless. So many years ago, we attended a leader's workshop where we actually walked on fire. As I followed my husband with blind faith onto the 50 feet of red hot coals, my 1st thought was *"what were we thinking!!!!"* But then I breathed out my fear and breathed in my courage. My brave actions solidified my brave thoughts. The flames did not burn our feet because our mind commanded our feet not to burn and our feet obeyed our thoughts. The 2000 degree heat and ash under my feet actually felt like cool moss between my toes. When we finished the faith walk both of our feet were untouched by the fire. UNBELIEV-ABLE!!! Now I knew once and for all that... BILL AND I COULD DO ANYTHING!!! Who you decide *TO BE* or *NOT TO BE* is limited only by you! Your life is the reflection of who you believe that you are! Are you a *"has been"* or a *"never was?"* It's never too late to be who you were born to be.

WHO ARE YOU?

BELIEVE IT or not!!!

Success has nothing to do with where you came from... the economy... or the weather. Success only comes from deep inside of each of us. You just have to dig deep enough to find it. Once you have discovered the power of the hidden treasures that lie dormant deep in the very core of your being, you can then pull up courage and confidence and faith to handle any challenge that you face. It's not about the amount of money that you have at the end of the week. It's about the "Feeling of Success" that you have when your week is over. The feeling of... "I came, I saw, I conquered." The feeling of... " This time I won. This is my time to be the head and not the tail... ". The very feeling of "This is it... " The feeling that God must have had after he created the universe and said... "It is good." Compare that to the feeling of losing... The feeling of being behind... The feeling of being helpless... Enough already! You get the point. Your emotions effect every cell in your body. Mind and body... physical and mental... are all connected. Money is worth something, but the "feeling" that you get by being successful is priceless!!! If everyone can agree that life is meant to be fruitful, if everyone can agree that the world is not against us, but for us, if everyone truly can believe the universe is on our side, then things will begin to change for everyone. When we finally give up the notion that we just have bad luck, watch what happens. When we finally truly believe that it is more natural to succeed rather than to fail, watch everything start to turn around in the right direction FOR EVERYONE! We all obviously do not desire normal jobs where we punch a time clock of 9 to 5.

We are not just workers trying to survive and pay our bills to get by. What a boring life that would be. We are all on the ride of a lifetime... reaching for the stars... Dream On!!! Your dream will always be challenged. Anyone who has ever lived and had a dream has faced the same challenges. For example, Martin Luther King was persecuted and betrayed because he dared to say "I have a dream." I believe people who produce passion usually are crowned or crucified. I'm not just a "Positive Pollyanna" who believes that life is just a bowl of cherries. Trust me. My dream is my philosophy... My philosophy is my heart and soul... My heart & soul is my life... I have been trampled and dragged through the mud, and you know what? I'm still successful. I'm becoming more successful day after day. I guess that's what some people would call a miracle. You must know who you are and what you live for. I am successful... Because...

I BELIEVE
IN MYSELF!!!.....

You can be successful if you believe you can be successful no matter what the people say. You can be healthy if you believe you can be healthy no matter what the doctors say. Believe in your dreams, have faith in your dreams..... "And faith is the evidence of things that are hoped for."

BELIEVE IT OR NOT!!

Chapter 12

TOP 10s

"I took the **first** footstep with a good **thought**...
I took the **second** footstep with a good **word**...
I took the **third** footstep with a good **deed**...
I then entered Paradise."

- Book of Arda

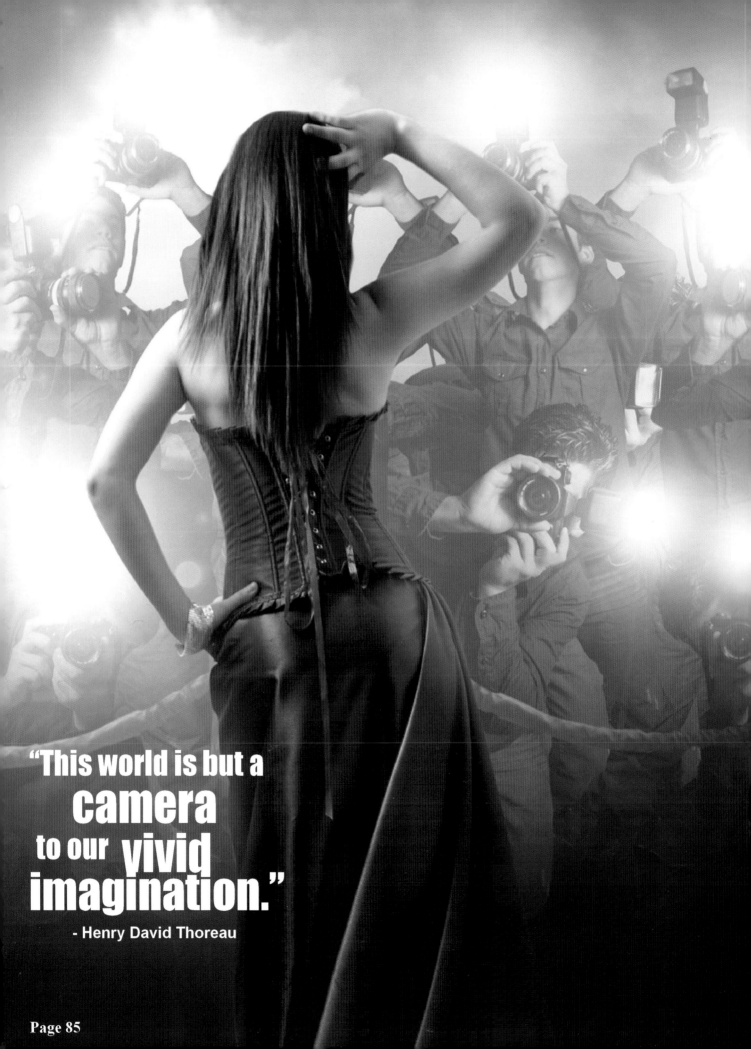

"This world is but a **camera** to our **vivid imagination.**"

- Henry David Thoreau

Top Ten
Things That Suck About Being A Model

1. Rejection at auditions
2. Stereotype of being shallow
3. Time on the road living alone in hotels
4. No regular 9 - 5 hours
5. No job security... one booking at a time
6. Being compared to someone prettier... taller... and thinner... etc
7. Physical appearance is scrutinized, analyzed, and criticized
8. Not appreciated for your intelligence
9. No corporate ladder for raises and promotions
10. The "Zoolander" image

Top Ten
Things That Rock About Being A Model

1. Seeing yourself in a magazine catalog or commercial
2. Traveling to exotic locations
3. Never the same job twice, never boring or monotonous
4. Amazing hourly & day rate salaries
5. Getting to wear the latest fashion as the job uniform
6. Working with top photographers, makeup artists... etc
7. Working for top clients in the film and fashion industry
8. No need to spend years training for a career unlike doctors
9. Being part of the iconic pop culture
10. LIVING YOUR DREAM!!!!

TOP TEN

AGENCIES

1. IMG	6. MARILYN
2. WOMEN	7. SUPREME
3. NEXT	8. TRUMP
4. FORD	9. ONE
5. DNA	10. NEW YORK MODELS

FASHION DESIGNERS

1. YVES SAINT LAURENT	6. ARMANI
2. VALENTINO	7. COCO CHANEL
3. VERSACE	8. HALSTON
4. RALPH LAUREN	9. DIOR
5. CALVIN KLEIN	10. MARC JACOBS

> "It's **OK** to have butterflies, just make them **fly in formation.**"
> Dr. Rob Gilbert

MODEL'S BAG ESSENTIALS

1. HAIR BRUSH
2. MAKE-UP
3. CELL PHONE
4. PORTFOLIO
5. RESUMĖ

6. CASTING CARDS
7. DAY PLANNER
8. DRESS SHIELDS
9. FAV BLACK HEELS
10. ENERGY SNACK

DIVAS OF THE DECADES

1. CHRISTIE BRINKLEY
2. TYRA BANKS
3. LAUREN HUTTON
4. CHRISTY TURLINGTON
5. NAOMI CAMPBELL
6. CINDY CRAWFORD

7. KATE MOSS
8. TWIGGY
9. HEIDI KLUM
10. GISELLE

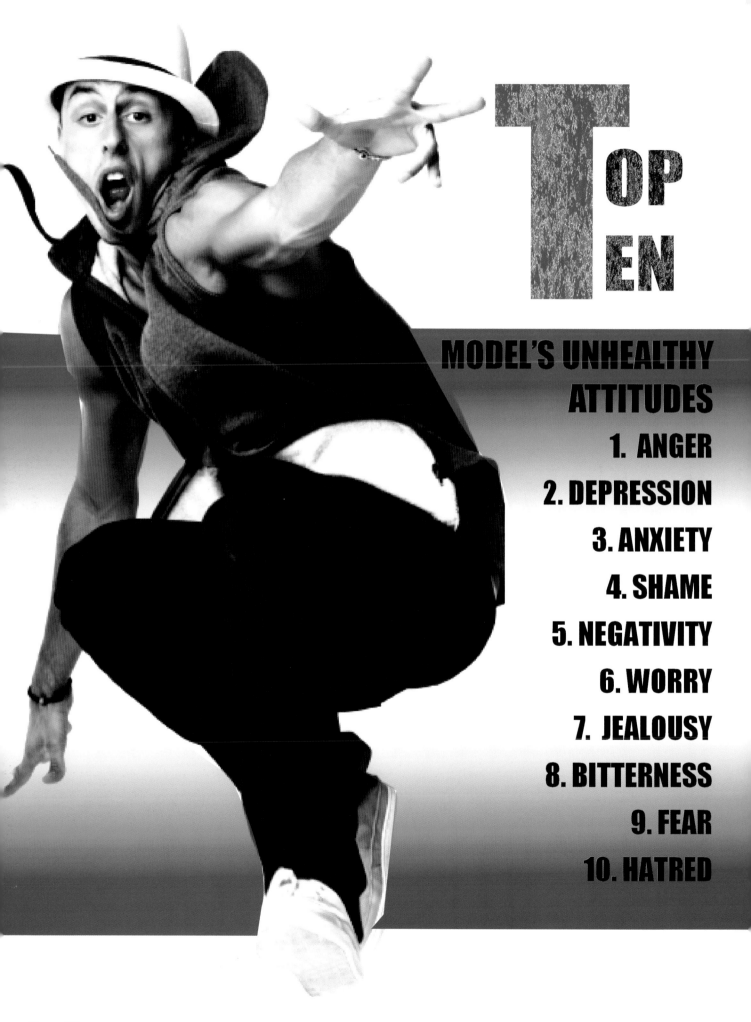

TOP TEN

MODEL'S UNHEALTHY ATTITUDES

1. ANGER
2. DEPRESSION
3. ANXIETY
4. SHAME
5. NEGATIVITY
6. WORRY
7. JEALOUSY
8. BITTERNESS
9. FEAR
10. HATRED

TOP TEN

MODEL'S HEALTHY ATTITUDES

1. INTEGRITY
2. CONTENTMENT
3. BALANCE
4. HAPPINESS
5. HUMILITY
6. JOY
7. PATIENCE
8. CREATIVITY
9. ADVENTURE
10. DETERMINATION

TOP TEN

DESIGN SCHOOLS

Before committing to a college career in fashion design, which is both costly and time consuming, it is best to begin with an apprenticeship or an intern program. Below is a list, in no particular order, of some of the top design schools.

1. Kent State University, Ohio (tuition $8,000/yr)

2. National Des Beaux-Arts, Paris (tuition internship)

3. Syracuse University, New York (tuition $30,000/yr)

4. Saint Martins College, London (tuition $14,000/yr)

5. Drexel University, Philadelphia (tuition $35,000/yr)

6. Art Institute of Chicago, Illinois ($1,000 per credit hour tuition)

7. Otis College of Art and Design, Los Angeles (tuition $30,000/yr)

8. Fashion Institute of Technology, New York (tuition $6,000/yr)

9. California College of The Arts, San Francisco (tuition $31,000/yr)

10. Savannah College of Art And Design, Georgia (tuition $27,000/yr)

TOP TEN

WISE CRACKS

1. Never give in. Never. Never. Never.
- Winston Churchill

2. When it comes to luck, you make your own.
- Bruce Springsteen

3. Where there is no struggle, there is no strength.
- Oprah Winfrey

4. Control your bad habits or they will control you.
- Benjamin Franklin

5 . You can neither win or lose if you don't run the race.
- David Bowie

6. Just do it.
- Nike Advertisement

7. Let nothing dim the light that shines from within.
- Maya Angelo

8. I believe that people can move things with their mind.
- Justin Timberlake

9. You must do the thing you think you cannot do.
- Elenor Roosevelt

10. The kingdom of God is within you.
- Jesus

Top en

POWER FOODS

1. ALMONDS	6. CABBAGE
2. FISH	7. GRAPEFRUIT
3. AVOCADO	8. GARLIC
4. SPINACH	9. BROWN RICE
5. BLUE BERRIES	10. JALAPENOS

TOP TEN

FOODS TO AVOID

1. SOFT DRINKS
2. PIES
3. PASTA
4. ICE CREAM
5. POTATO CHIPS

6. PIZZA
7. CANDY BARS
8. WHITE BREAD
9. FRIED FOODS
10. MAYONNAISE

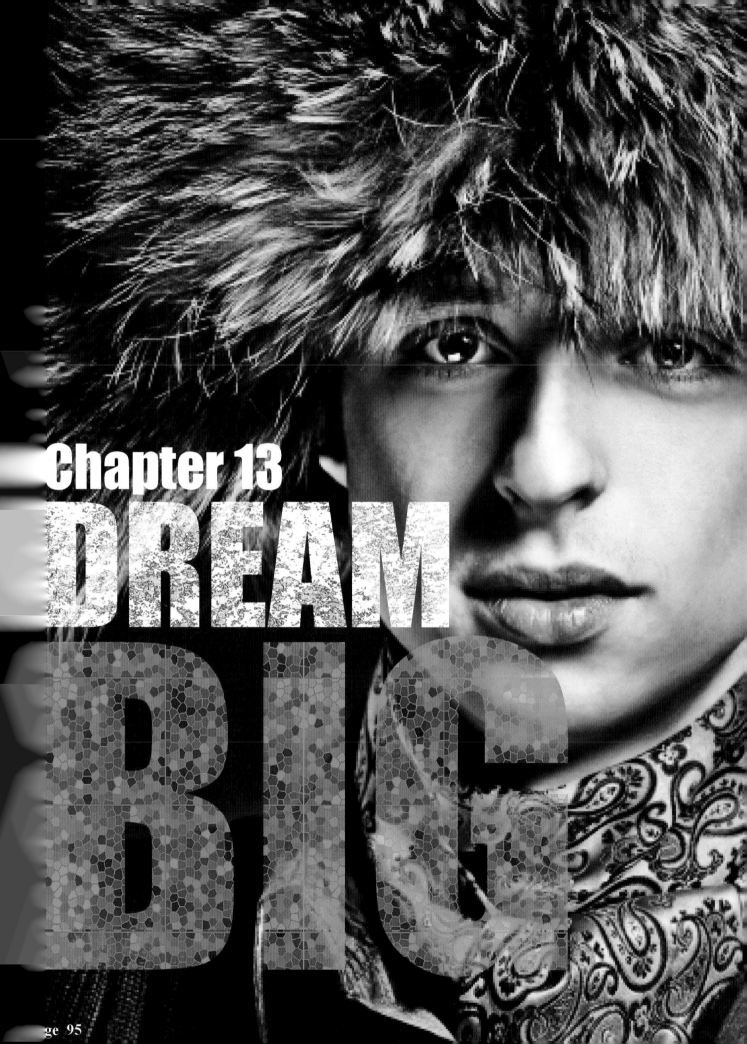

Chapter 13
DREAM BIG

"If you don't **dream big,** there's no use dreaming. If you don't **have faith,** there's nothing worth believing."

-Justin Bieber

"IMAGINE..." John Lennon

Be the mastermind behind your life

There are two different ways to see. One is called sight. That is created by your eyeballs. The other is called vision that is created by your mind. Sight is what you see now, in the present. It is what is in front of your face. Where as, vision is what is seen in the future. It is what your mind can imagine. Before there was the Internet, Bill Gates had a vision of a whole new electronic world. He used his imagination and creativity to bring it into our eyesight. Before there was the light bulb, Thomas Edison envisioned it, imagined it and spent his entire life developing his dream to bring light to the darkness. Before we went to the moon, John Kennedy envisioned it and challenged America to achieve the impossible. In my own example, years before I had the sight of my children with my eyeballs.... I had a vision of them in my mind and in my imagination. Even as a young girl, I would play with baby dolls and fantasize about being a mother. Years later, as a young couple, Bill and I would dream of having children. Then one day I turned around, and there they were... just as I imagined them to be.

Catwalk Productions existed for years and years in my mind, way before the first model ever walked the runway. Through the years, our models walked on make shift stages, such as bags of birdseed with a ply-wood over the top. However, I never stopped dreaming of a beautiful stage with runway lights. I still remember the first time my son, Doug, came to me and drew out the plan that he had envisioned for our new stage with silver trussing. One of my greatest thrills now is to watch great designs emerge on T-shirts, books, brochures, and posters that all come out of the mind and imagination of my daughter, April. When my son, Lance, was 6 years old, I sat our on our back porch and watched him 'invision' building a baseball stadium in our backyard. He carefully mapped out the playing field and dreamed of hitting home runs over our backyard fence. The day ended abruptly when he cut a big hole in his foot chopping wood with an ax to build and construct his bleachers. But guess what? We didn't stop dreaming. Years later, Lance developed the plans for our current production and built the program with the same enthusiasm that he had built his baseball stadium. Lisa, my oldest child, who has been my right arm in life for 33 years, still has our original notebook book where we kept our rosters and records years before computers came along. We began with a weekly budget of $35. Since our corporate office was in our living room and all of my kids worked for free, we didn't have many expenses. We always had enough left over at the end of the week to all go to Dairy Queen and spend our profit. Thirty years later and now staffed with over 100 employees, our dream is still growing strong. I also always taught my kids when they were young, to dream about their future marriages and to visualize or pray about their future life partners. Johnny, Ashley, and Danielle are living proof that my kids have very vivid imaginations! So what is the point? I encourage all of you to set goals. Your goal is your vision. You must see it in your mind everyday. You must dream it in

your heart all the time. It must become your passion. When I was 40 years old, I delivered my 5th child. Even though the doctors doubted that my body could handle the pregnancy. My vision of my little "Amazing Grace" carried me through. Almost 20 years later, she is working by my side, all grown up. So what is your dream? You must pursue it with all of your strength. Meeting your goal is not your reward. The end result is not your joy. The journey to the vision IS YOUR LIFE!

ENJOY THE JOURNEY!

The day by day path to your vision is the dream unfolding before your eyes. Seize the moment. Look who is beside you on your journey. Focus on the positive. Be grateful! Some people choose to only see what is in front of them. Don't waste your vision by imagining bad things happening in your future, That's called worrying or fear. Don't waste your vision by plotting revenge or making plans to get even. That is called a complete waste of time. Begin right now to create a vision of what you want in your mind... Good health... Good fortune... Whatever, just be very specific. Vague vision, just like poor eyesight will cause you to run into walls. Do you have a vision for your daily schedule? What is your goal for every day? Don't waste time. Where do you see yourself living eventually? What does your house look like? Is it a mansion? Why not? DREAM BIG!

think the thing to do is to
enjoy the ride
while you are on it."
-Johnny Depp

You gotta Flow to Grow

Some people seem to flow through life and other people obviously struggle every day. People who flow smile a lot. People who struggle, complain constantly. People who flow seem to be anointed with the talents they need to accomplish their tasks. People who struggle blame other people or circumstances for their inability to produce. Lebron James and Carrie Underwood are both examples of people who flow. Both of them work by the sweat of their brow... But neither of them struggle to produce. Carrie is on the road constantly and spends long hours in the recording studio, but then simply opens her mouth and her talent flows. Lebron runs up and down the court under tremendous pressure to produce, but it seems that he welcomes the opportunity to shoot a three pointer at the ending buzzer. It's almost as if, the more he sweats, the more he flows.

Working hard and enjoying what you do is flowing. Working hard and being miserable about what you do is struggling. So what is your talent? Are you a natural on stage? Are you a gifted photographer? Just remember to flow with what feels right to you. One of the greatest lessons that I have learned during my 6 decades on this beautiful blue planet is to be content and satisfied within myself wherever I am. Places, people, and circumstances change every day, like the white clouds quickly passing in the sky. But my contentment to be in the moment of whatever I am doing, wherever I am, is like the blue part of the sky that doesn't move or change. I have lived in a shack. I have lived in a mansion. Different houses... same me. I have felt the ecstasy of holding a newborn baby and felt the birth pains of labor within the same hour. Different emotions... same me. I have known the thrill of victory and the agony of defeat. Different results... same me.

> "As your faith is strengthened, you will find that there is no longer the need to have the sense of control. Things will flow and you will learn to flow with them much to your delight and benefit." -Wingate Paine

Close your eyes... And breathe deeply for 3 minutes. 3 times a day. Breathe in strength, health, success and joy. Breathe out anger, dysfunction, disease and discontent.

You gotta Thrive to Survive

One of the most difficult tasks I have faced as being a leader is to motivate people who are not content. People who are happy one day and sad the next day are hard to lead. People who are content one day and bored the next day are impossible to satisfy. Fortunately, those people are usually here one day and gone the next day... always searching. still looking for contentment. Maybe their next job will be easier? Probably not! Maybe their next relationship will make them happy? Probably not! People who are not content usually become "energy vampires" by trying to suck the life out of their friends and family... always whining... always complaining... always looking for greener grass on the other side of the fence. People who are content are peaceful, relaxed, and motivated right where they are. Models who start this industry looking to find happiness rarely find satisfaction from their job. Someone who is not content within themselves, will never be content with fame or fortune. People who are not content struggle every day. People who are not content rarely have a positive personality. People who are not content poison the air around them like a bad odor in the room. People who are not content tend to make everyone around them discontented also. Simply find your contentment first, then find your place in the film and fashion industry.

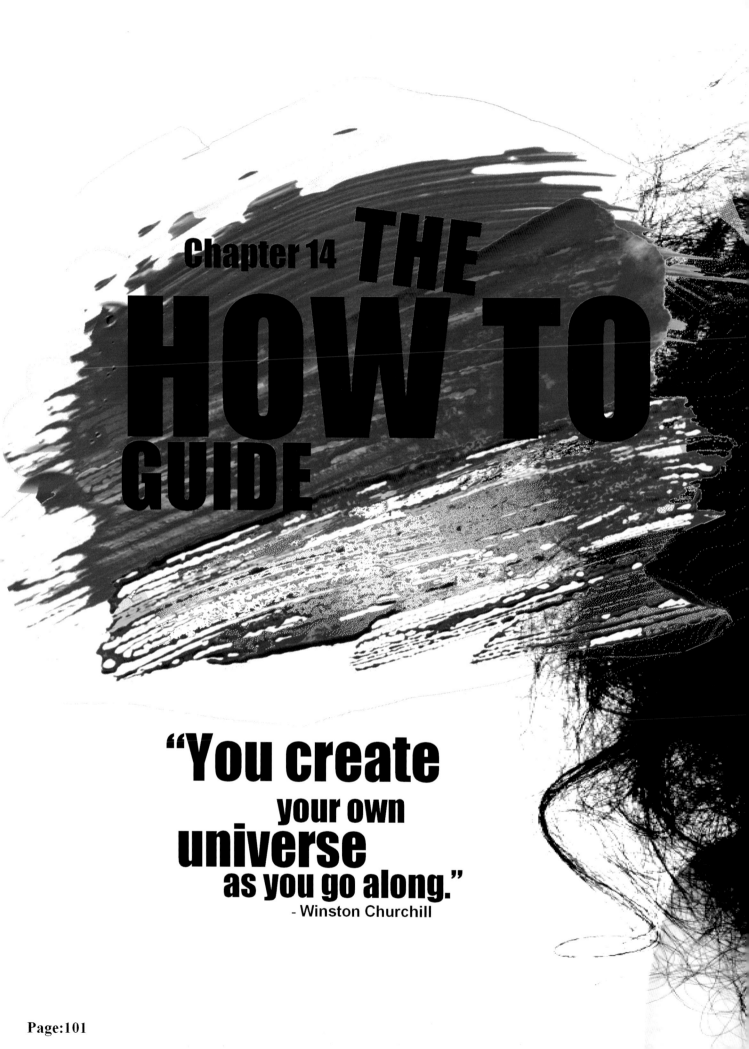

Chapter 14 THE HOW TO GUIDE

"You create your own universe as you go along."
- Winston Churchill

HOW TO WIN
AN AUDITION

1. Take constructive criticism.

2. Make eye contact with clients.

3. Have a positive "can do" attitude.

4. Demonstrate poise, personality and self confidence.

5. Relax and have fun.

6. Work another job to pay the bills, so you don't appear desperate.

7. Dress code is business casual... blazer with tank and jeans or simple black dress.

8. Present a great casting card, headshot, and resumé

9. Greet client with friendly smile, warm attitude and firm handshake.

10. Be prepared to take notes and instructions on a day planner.

11. Be unique and different. Try to stand out.

12. Speak slowly and distinctly.

13. Never let them see you sweat!

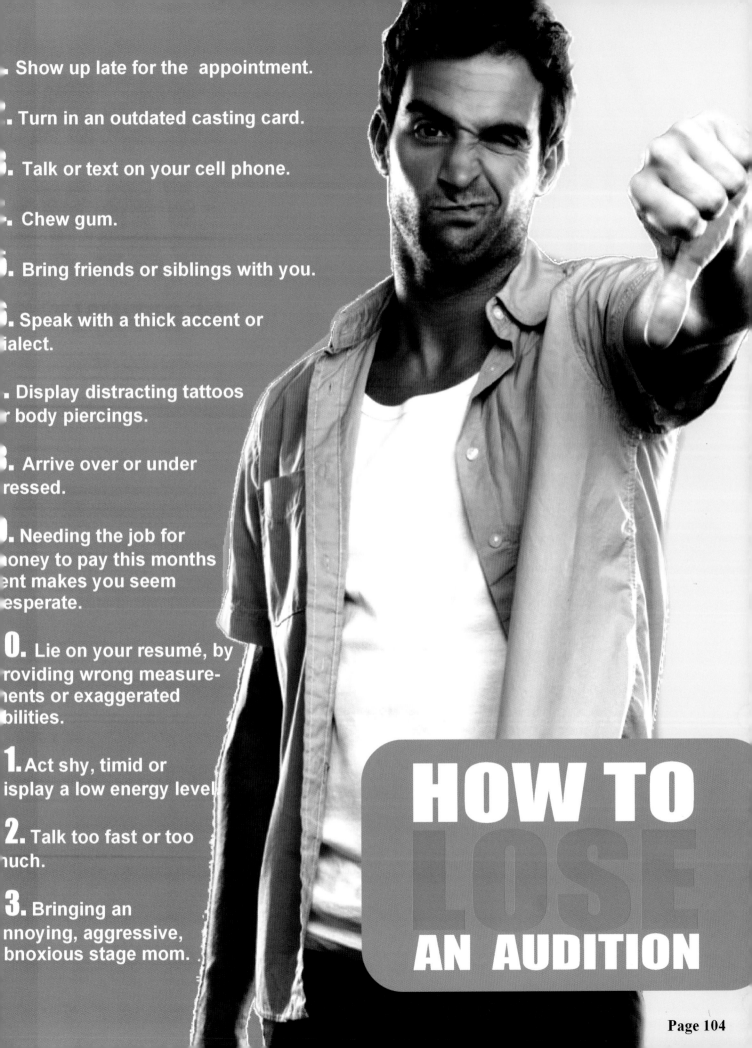

1. Show up late for the appointment.

2. Turn in an outdated casting card.

3. Talk or text on your cell phone.

4. Chew gum.

5. Bring friends or siblings with you.

6. Speak with a thick accent or dialect.

7. Display distracting tattoos or body piercings.

8. Arrive over or under dressed.

9. Needing the job for money to pay this months rent makes you seem desperate.

10. Lie on your resumé, by providing wrong measurements or exaggerated abilities.

11. Act shy, timid or display a low energy level.

12. Talk too fast or too much.

13. Bringing an annoying, aggressive, obnoxious stage mom.

HOW TO LOSE AN AUDITION

How To ROCK THE RUNWAY

MODELS HAVE TWO MISSIONS ON THE CATWALK:

A. SELL THE CLOTHES   B. ENTERTAIN THE AUDIENCE

1. Begin by drawing all attention to your face, letting the audience know immediately who is in charge.

2. Look fierce and valiant like you can conquer the world.

3. Walk with your feet to the beat of the music.

4. Control all body parts precisely and distinctly... especially the arms.

5. Swing the arms gently from the elbows, not the shoulders.

6. Say to yourself right before going on stage...

"I AM A MODEL."

7. Take your time...
stop occasionally and strike a pose.

8. Consistently, create moods and emotions as you
seize the moment and work the runway... such as:

Playful	Shy	Playful
Happy	Sexy	Sassy
Mysterious	Flirty	Aloof

9. Interact with the fashions by modeling the garment

Touch the sleeves	Wiggle the tie
Pull down on shirt	Hands in pocket
Flare the skirt	Grab the collar

10. Be creative and unique. "Wow" the crowd.

HOW TO MAKE

First, make a list of all of your hobbies, talents and abilities that would be considered a marketable skill.

Stuntman	Magician	Break Dancing	Taekwondo
Scuba	Martial Arts	Sign Language	Boston Accent
Singer	Jump Rope	Swimmer	Ballet
Hip Hop	Juggle	Gymnastics	Robotics
Runway	Motorcycle	Choreography	Boxer
Jazz	Rapper	Live Mannequin	Speak French
Tap	Wrestler	Southern Accent	Dramatic Actor
Clown	Speak Spanish	New York Accent	Wrestler
Choir Vocal	Comedy Actor	Line Dance	Animal Trainer
Poet	Guitar	Voice Over	Piano
Roller Skate	Public Speaker	Ice Skate	Spokes model
Baseball	Snow Ski	Life Guard	Surf
Tennis	Play	Community Theater	Football
Yodel	Japanese Accent	Japanese Language	Yoga
DJ	Marching Band	Auctioneer	Majorette
Awards	Song Writer	College Degree	High School Diploma
Aerobics	Race Car Driver	Rodeo	Sky Diver
Soccer	Trampoline	English Accent	Jamaican Accent
Rock Wall	Horse Rider	Clown	Cheerleader
Drama Club	Water Ski	Skate Board	

Even though a resume` is the proper platform to brag about yourself, remember to be honest about your abilities and do not exaggerate your talents. Just because you rode a pony at the fair, does not mean that you are a skilled horse back rider. The fact that you took Spanish in high school one year, does not mean that you are bilingual. "Taco Bell" is not a Spanish word!

A resume should also list your limitations or weaknesses, which a casting director should be aware, such as:

Asthma	Lactose Intolerant	Bee Sting Reaction
Diabetic	Snake Phobia	Allergies
Non-Swimmer	Can't Speak English	Afraid of Heights

A RESUME'

HOW TO
WORK THE
CAMERA

"Don't just stand there...
Let's get to it!
Strike a pose....
There's nothing to it."
-MADONNA

One pose is actually 3 or 4 different poses of body parts put together.

Models must multi task with

Facial expressions, Feet stance. Twist of torso, Arm position

Practice different moods and emotions in front of your mirror developing a variety of expressions using the facial features. Raise the eye brows, direct the look of the eyes, tilt the head, pout the lips.

Develop at least 10 ways
to smile

Sexy... Grin... Laugh... Smirk... Shy... Smug....

A prepared model will show up for a shoot with at least 50 planned and practiced poses.

Makeup must be bigger than life and applied heavier than normal to handle close-ups.

Yoga, stretching and pilates all help the body achieve the flexibility and fitness needed to twist and turn the body.

Choose a hairstyle that is versatile and can be styled multiple ways.

"You better work it!"... is not just a popular song about modeling. It is the truth. Photo shoots can last for hours under hot lights with hundreds of poses and dozens of wardrobe changes.

FASHION PHOTOGRAPHY 101

Find your beauty.

Look in the mirror. Find your strongest features. Decide what's your best and worst feature. Everyone has things they don't like about themselves... The key is to accept what you don't like and focus on what you do like. The criticism about Cindy Crawford's infamous mole could have kept her out of the industry. But she turned the obstacle into an opportunity. The thing that makes you feel different than everyone else, can become the thing that makes you unique. Cindy turned her mole into a "beauty mark" that is now her trade mark. Girls around the world penciled in "beauty marks" of their own to look just like Cindy.

Accentuate it.

Next accentuate your strengths and hide your weaknesses. If your have gorgeous hair, do swinging hair poses that draw attention to that area... If you love your eyes, wear a color that makes them pop. Learn your best angles, facial expressions, and poses that accentuate your strengths and hide your weaknesses.

Capture it.

Now get ready to deliver! Confidence is one of the main components to being photogenic. That confidence will come naturally as you gain experience in front of the camera.

WORK IT BABY, WORK IT!

POSING
Is All About Your Face

A modeling career is a smorgasbord of many careers rolled into one. First and foremost, a model is simply a performer. We perform everyday on stage... on the catwalk and in front of the camera. If you do not like the spotlight, modeling is not for you. If you are shy or timid, do not become a model.

The most important part of posing is a model's facial expression. Regardless of the pose, lighting, angle, and cropping... the model's face controls the mood and feeling of the photo. The secret to this industry is not just to get hired by a major client.... but to get RE-hired over and over again, thus making this an actual career. Clients re-hire models that are easy to work with and models that know their job. Major clients spend countless hours creating and developing their line or product. Their product represents them as an artist of their craft. A model represents their product. You are the face portraying their vision. Are you starting to see why models are paid so well? Models are not just a pretty face. But rather, models are talented professionals that can act or play a part. A MODEL SHOULD CATCH YOUR EYE WITH THEIR POSE and TELL A STORY WITH THEIR EYES. Good models force you to feel an emotion because of their expression. Model's sell products. Never forget that a model's body is a coat hanger, and a model's face is a frame for make-up. Model's entertain while modeling and selling at the same time.

IDEA

CHRISTMAS MORNING

SMILE

BORED

LAUGH

"I think **happiness** is what **makes you pretty.**

Period. Happy people are beautiful. They become like a mirror and reflect that happiness."
-Drew Barrymore

Doing two thing at once... This does not come naturally. For anyone! It takes practice and hard work to perfect your craft. The easiest way to memorize poses is to create a pose portfolio. Go through fashion magazines and search for poses that catch your eye, especially models that are "doing their job" and drawing attention to their advertisement. Then take those pages and make your own pose portfolio. Keep it in front of your mirror and practice the poses and facial expressions as much as possible. Develop versatility. As the model below demonstrates, the poses can be pretty simple and similar but the facial expression makes each look different and unique. Parents should practice with their kids and develop key words that trigger the pose in the child's mind. Example Keywords: (follow the images from bottom of the van.images below from left to right) IDEA, CHRISTMAS MORNING, SMILE, BORED, LAUGHING, THINKING, OPEN MOUTH LAUGH, MADAND FLIRTY.

THINKING

MAD

OPEN MOUTH LAUGH

FLIRTY

EXPRESS YOURSELF

Practice and memorize these facial expressions to use on your next shoot.

SURPRISED	SWEET	GIDDY	WINK
LAUGH	SHOCKED	"HOME ALONE"	SERIOUS
MAD	HAPPY	SCREAM	BORED
SHY	SNEAKY	CRAZY	FLIRTY
THINKING	IDEA	EXCITED	ANGRY
SEXY	FIERCE	ROCK STAR	SILLY
CHEESY	GIGGLING	CONFUSED	SAD

"As a young child, I would lock myself in my bathroom for hours, making facial expressions in my mirror."
-Jim Carrey

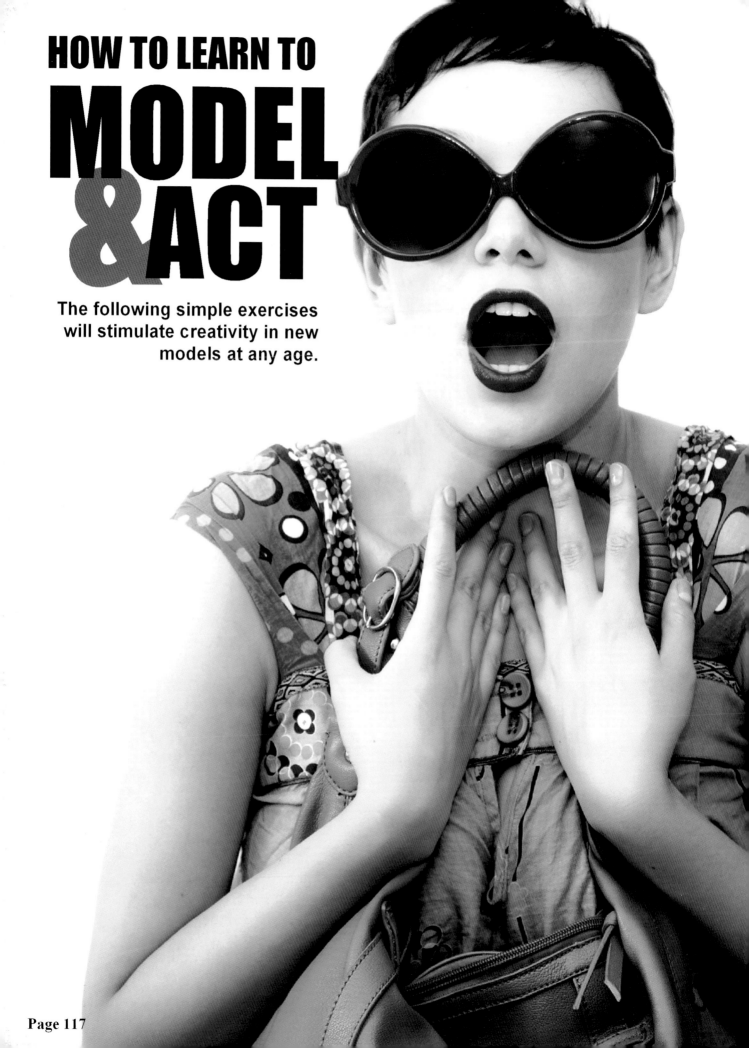

HOW TO LEARN TO
MODEL
&ACT

The following simple exercises will stimulate creativity in new models at any age.

CHARADES IMPROVISATION

An actor has 3 instruments. The face, the body and the voice.
Use your instruments to create the scene.

I AM Taking A Shower	I AM Freezing Cold	I AM A Tiger
I AM Eating A Banana	I AM A Eating Spaghetti	I AM A Juggler
I AM Watching A Scary Movie	I AM A Race Car Driver	I AM Sky Diving

TOILET PAPER FASHION SHOW

Divide into 2 teams. One person is the model. The other is the fashion designer. The designer uses toilet paper as fabric and unwinds the roll around the model creating a unique "fashion design." Afterwards have a toilet paper fashion show and judge the best designs.

MEMORIZING PRACTICE

This will improve a model's memory skills for memorizing lines and scripts. This is a warm up to get the brain moving.

1. Sit in a circle.
2. 1st person creates a rhythm such as "Snap snap" with their fingers.
3. The second person repeats "snap snap" and adds "clap clap" with their hands.
4. The next person repeats the first two and then adds a whistle sound.
5. It continues around the circle until someone forgets and misses the rhythm. They are then out and it skips to the next person.

BROWN BAG THEATER

Divide the group into 3 teams. Take 3 brown bags and place 10 random items in each bag. Be creative and put different and unusual items in each. For example: in 1 bag place a dog leash, In the 2nd bag, put a wrapped present, and in the 3rd bad put an alarm clock. Continue up to 10 items in each bag. The groups challenge s to create a short skit using the items as props to create a plot with dialogue.

MEMORY EXERCISE

Take a model's bag filled with model accessories and place the items on a tray. Allow a 2 minutes period where young models are given the chance to examine the items shape and size by touching and feeling them. Use items such as a scarf, a cell phone, a brush, a lip gloss, etc... After the 2 minute study period, put the items back into the model's bag. Then have the models race to list the items from memory. The first one to successfully name all items correctly... WINS!

T-SHIRT PROJECT RUNWAY

Just like the popular TV show, have a contest to see who can take a simple t-shirt and create the best fashion look. Layer it... bedazzle it... cut it up... twist it... tie it... be creative and most of all, don't forget, accessorize it.

MAKE BELIEVE PROPS

Take a random item and take turns creating it into a pretend prop.
Example: a broomstick can be...

1. A Horse	2. A Microphone	3. A Guitar

How to understand the BUSINESS of SHOW BUSINESS

Unlike most careers that require years of college and thousands of dollars for school and training, there is no formal degree or diploma required to land a job in the film or fashion industry. However, there are very good modeling workshops, acting classes, and industry seminars that are fantastic sources of education. As a general rule, dancers attend dancing schools, musicians take music lessons and it's usually a good idea for a singer to hire a vocal coach in order to develop their talent. All models must have a portfolio and all actors must have a headshot. Casting cards and resumes are required at all auditions. A painter must have his own ladder, a beautician must have her own scissors, and a professional tennis player purchases his own tennis racket. Likewise models pay for their own portfolios. AGENCIES DO NOT PAY FOR MODEL SUPPLIES. If there is ever an advancement for photos, the model is always required to pay it back. Find a great photographer at a reasonable rate. Industry standards vary and include black and white head shots to color composites. Always be sure your portfolio and resumé are current and up to date. Photos will eventually be replaced with tear sheets as your resume grows. A cheerleader would not show up at a game without pom poms, and a model should never be at a casting or audition without casting cards. And finally, and most importantly, do not quit your day job to become a model! No career happens over night. Every vocation takes time to develop. Don't pursue modeling to pursue fame and fortune. Pursue it for the joy of the job and not for money. Teachers teach because they love children and nurses work because of their heart to help people. If you don't have a passion for fashion, STAY OUT OF THE BUSINESS! Models who are broke, appear pitiful and desperate at auditions. Most models begin their career as a part time model and as a part time waiter... or any other job that pays the bills, until their modeling career can fully support them. Remember over 50% of card carrying SAG actors are still only part time employees.

> "Make sure you are passionate about your craft and able to handle rejection. I've been told "no" a lot in this town."
>
> -Selena Gomez

> ## "Happiness depends upon ourselves."
> ### -Aristotle

HOW TO
REACH YOUR GOALS

STEP 1:
FOCUS

A magnifying glass held still in one place over paper can create a fire. If it moves around aimlessly, nothing will happen. Focus all of your thought and actions in one direction. Quit skipping around from one thing to another. Concentrate.... Focus.

STEP 2:
BE SPECIFIC

Don't just say, I want to make money. Write down a dollar amount as a goal. Don't say you want to lose weight. Write down the number of pounds exactly and the date that you intend to achieve your goal.

STEP 3:
DIVIDE & CONQUER

We all have eaten an entire cow! How did we do it? One bite at a time. Every goal that you set should have daily, weekly and monthly goals. Its hard to imagine losing 60 lbs, but if you set a time limit of 6 months, it can be broken down to 10 lbs a month. And each month can be broken down into 2½ lbs a week. 60 lbs then becomes do-able.

HOW TO MAKE A DEMO
ARE YOU READY?

YouTube is the current most popular launching pad for new models and actors to audition for national exposure. Stars like Justin Bieber, MegynGraceLIVE and ICarly were discovered demonstrating their talent and ability on YouTube. Before the invention of the Internet and the World Wide Web, rookie models had to travel around the country to audition in person at casting calls. Thank goodness, those days are gone forever. In today's high tech society, castings and auditions are emailed and downloaded instantly. No more traveling for days and waiting in long lines for hours. Casting directors can see many more contestants electronically than personally. Top scouts for TV shows now look through YouTube demo tapes, instead of the old fashioned ways of scouting new faces at airports, restaurants, and on the street. Try these sample scripts and see what happens. Remember to demonstrate poise and personality, as well as charm and charisma. It's not what you say, it's how you say it.

COMMERCIAL:

Do you have a passion for fashion? Check out what's hot... and what's not at _____

(favorite store).

MOVIE SCRIPT:

Dad, why do we have to move to Chicago anyway? My whole life is here. My friends... my school.... my home... everything! This is my life too.

TV SCRIPT:

Did you hear, Bailey? I got the part! I can't believe it. I'm actually going to California. OK breathe .... breathe. Pinch me and see if I'm dreaming. Ouch!!! Oh, my gosh... it's real, i'm going to Hollywood... I'm going to Hollywood!

LIVE MANNEQUIN/MUSIC VIDEO:
Sing or dance to a song such as:

Sexy Back - Justin Timberlake
Someone Like You-Adele
Best of Both Worlds-Hannah Montana

Hips Don't Lie - Shakira
Baby- Justin Beiber
Our Song - Taylor Swift
Yeah! - Usher

FASHION SHOW

Wear your most trendy stylish outfit and model it on camera. Try to show a variety of facial expressions with creative body poses. Coordination and rhythm must also be demonstrated.

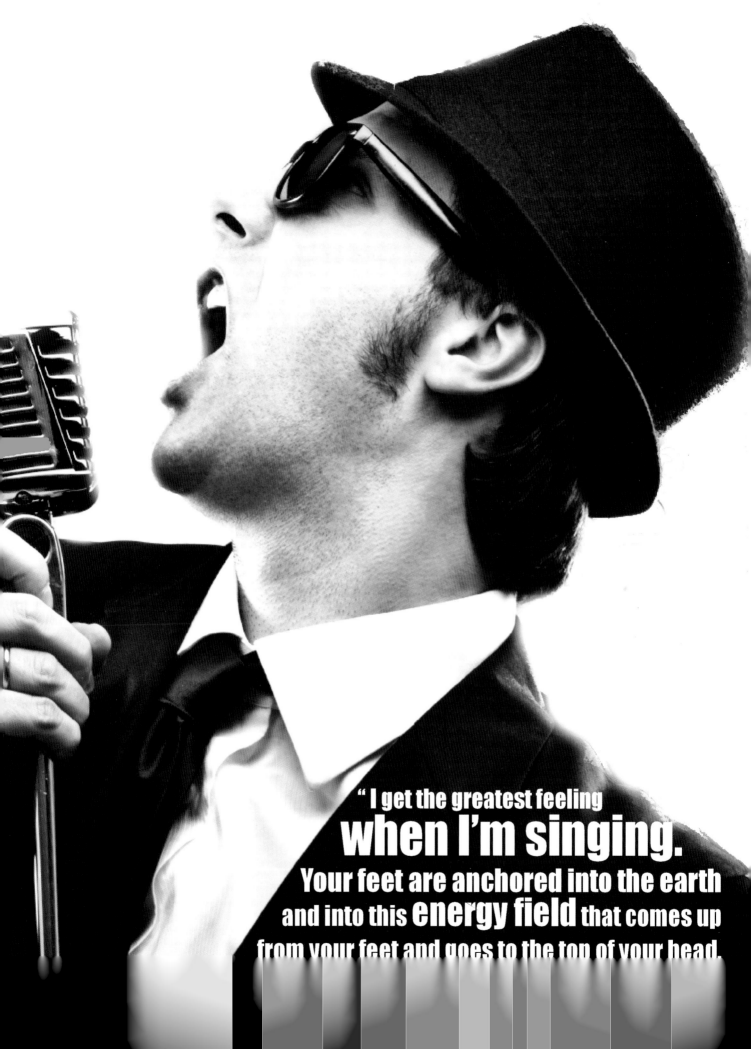

" I get the greatest feeling **when I'm singing.** Your feet are anchored into the earth and into this **energy field** that comes up from your feet and goes to the top of your head.

HOW TO: LIVE MANNEQUIN
FREEZE MODELING IN STORE WINDOWS

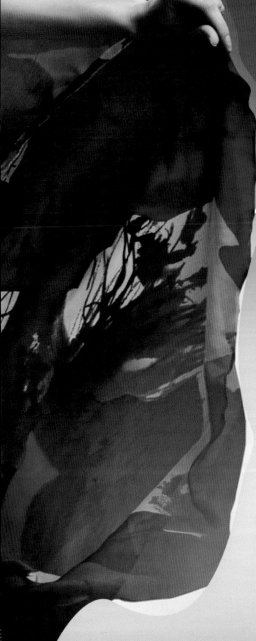

JOB OBJECTIVE

1. To draw a crowd to the store window
2. To pose to enhance the fit and feel of the garment
3. To be the focal point of the store.

TIPS FOR SUCCESS

1. Be robotic, but not stiff

2. Pose the arms away from the body with wrists flexed backward.

3. Never hold a pose for more than 30 seconds.

4. The head tilts left, the torso twists right, the legs tilt left or vice versa.

5. Be unique and creative with fluid motion of poses and movement.

6. Remember to over exaggerate facial expressions and change faces with every pose.

7. Re-hang and return all merchandise to rack promptly.

8. Don't bring friends and family into a store with you while working.

HOW TO:
HELP YOUR ASPIRING MODEL
ARE YOU A "STAGE MOM?"

There are many free resources available to the aspiring young talent. Community theater, choirs, mall fashion boards, and school drama clubs are all breeding grounds for rookies to develop their skills. Parents should never take a child seriously who says that they want to be a model, but who are not willing to put time and effort into learning and growing as a performer. Many parents... excuse me, ALL parents think their child is beautiful! Get over it. Pretty faces are a dime a dozen, Before moving your family to Hollywood, it's a good idea to start locally. Every career has a ladder and you must work your way up. You don't join the army as a general, at the top... you join the army as a private, at the bottom. You don't go to your 1st audition to be a star, you go to land a role as a movie extra. Model searches, dance competitions and acting contests also will give parents a measuring tool to prove their child's commitment and dedication, as well as their ability.

All parents who are serious about helping their children succeed as a model, must develop the same spirit of sacrifice and dedication as is expected of the child. Parents of young athletes spend hours sitting in the hot sun watching their kids win and lose in Little League. Families of young gymnasts spend years rearranging their schedules around competitions. Parents of models should never complain about required time and effort to aid the dreams and aspirations of their children. An immediate red flag to a casting director, is a stage mom who is pushy arrogant and impatient. Many careers of talented kids have been lost due to parents who are not supportive. I've seen dads complain about the time they wasted when their kids forgot their line and blew an audition. I've seen moms mad because the casting is two hours away, and gas is $3 a gallon. Parents must understand that modeling is an activity that allows families to have a common goal to work together. Modeling should be a hobby that is fun for the family and not a pressure cooker for kids to succeed. Kids usually strike out a hundred times before they hit a home run, and likewise kids usually lose auditions before they win them. Modeling is not a path for your child to make you rich quick. Look at the families of Micheal Jackson and Lindsey Lohan. Learn from their mistakes and enjoy the journey. Visualize your child one day winning an Oscar... standing in front of the audience of millions thanking you for being "The Wind Beneath Their Wings." Most kids can handle the wins and losses. It's usually the parents who ride an emotional roller coaster. Being happy when things are easy and angry when things are tough, will not only destroy your child's dream, but it will also hurt your relationship. Therefore, you must be 100% committed to this journey win or lose and for as long as it takes. It's better not to begin, than start and quit along the way.

"I am determined to be cheerful and happy. I have learned that happiness is created by our disposition and not by our circumstances."

-Mrs. George Washington

Do you have a PASSION

Which of these divas are your role model? They are as different as the colors of the rainbow. Don't just wear clothes. Dress to impress. Make a fashion statement. None of these ladies set out to change the world. They were just being themselves, integrating their personality with their wardrobe. Try it yourself. You are as unique as a snowflake. Follow your passion and see what you create.

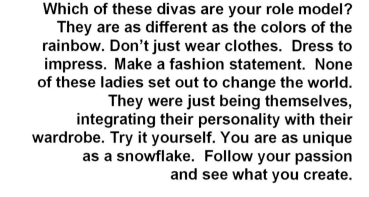

Jackie Kennedy

became a fashion icon when she walked the political, red carpets in her form fitting suits with pillow hats. She created the sophisticated look of the "Camelot" fashion era.

Marilyn Monroe

became a modeling legend when she struck the right pose in a white flared dress over a New York exhaust vent. Fifty years after her death, people are still in awe of her glamour and sex appeal.

Lady GAGA

proves today that any of us can be "FASHIONISTAS." She epitomizes the fashion culture today which is anything goes. Her raw meat gowns and her metal head dresses have created an atomic explosion in couture. Now its ok to wear sequins in the daytime. Socks with sandals. no problem. Whatever is right for you is right for fashion.

for FASHION?

Mary Tyler Moore

changed *the look* of American women's fashion forever when she played the role of Laura on the Dick Van Dyke Show. Never before had a woman been filmed in a TV show wearing anything but dresses. She became the first female to dare to be filmed wearing pants. Unbelievable but true.

Princess Diana

stole the hearts of millions, as she become the people's princess in her fairy tale wedding dress. Even though she did not live happily ever after herself, she inspired a whole generation to believe in fairy tales again and grow up to be just like her.

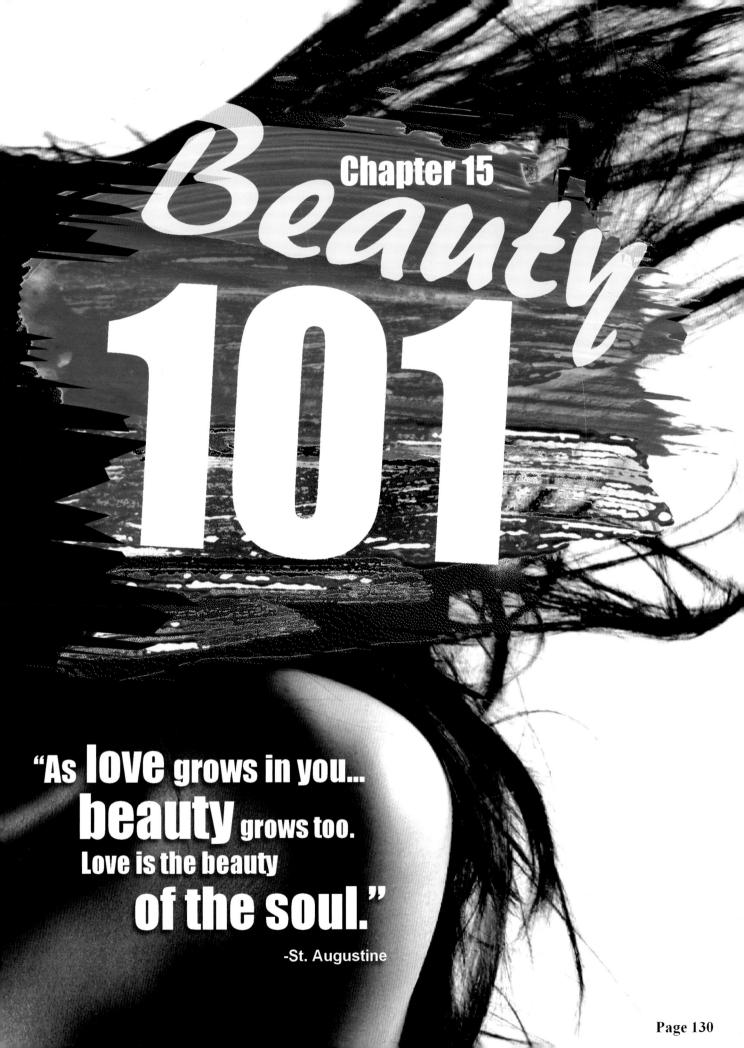

Chapter 15

Beauty 101

"As love grows in you...
beauty grows too.
Love is the beauty
of the soul."

-St. Augustine

BEAUTY

HAIR

1. Static electricity in your hair? No problem. Spray hairspray on your brush and your locks will calm down.

2. Don't blow dry hair when dripping wet. First towel dry thoroughly, and you will cut down on heat damage to your hair.

3. Stinky hair from food or cigarette smoke? Just rub a fabric softener sheet through your locks and the smell is gone!

4. If your colored hair turns green after swimming, rinse it with tomato juice to return hair to original color.

5. If your hair high lights are too brassy or too harsh, shampoo with dish soap until you can get back to the salon to redo.

6. To keep curls from flattening while you rest, sleep with a silk or satin pillow case. Curls will bounce back easily the next morning.

7. No more tangles! While you are still in the shower, comb through your hair with the conditioner on it. When you get out, the tangles will be gone.

8. If your hair has fallen flat like a souffle', turn your head upside down, shoot a volumizer at the roots and brush vigorously. Flip it back over and go.

9. Use a small amount of baby powder in your roots to absorb hairs excess oil between shampoos.

10. Rub raw apple cider vinegar on the scalp to eliminate dandruff.

11. In between coloring, use dark eye shadows on a tooth brush to quickly cover gray hair at the roots.

NAILS

1. Create a french manicure by drawing with a white eye pencil coloring under the nail.

SECRETS

SKIN

1. Tea tree oil is a natural antiseptic for blemishes.

2. Don't wax your upper lip. Bleach it instead. No girl wants mustache stubble!

3. Out of blush? Make-Up emergency? Just rub a dab of lipstick on your cheeks. It gives the same effects!

4. Use hair conditioner to shave your legs to moisturize the skin and prevent razor burn.

5. Stinky sweaty feet? Soak feet in Epsom salt water or apple cider vinegar water and feel the magic!

6. Put baking soda in boots or shoes to absorb excess moisture and odor.

7. When applying perfume, spray some under your hair, and watch more people notice your aroma.

8. Wash make-up brushes often to prevent bacteria build up which can cause break outs.

12. Eating an apple a day will usually neutralize bad breathe.

13. Drink 4 to 6 bottles of water daily.

14. Stop 3 times a day and take 10 deep breaths.

15. Never sleep with your make-up still on.

16. Practice good posture by holding your shoulders back. It's a natural breast lift.

LIPS

1. Lipstick with brown undertones will look flat in a photo. Not a good choice.

2. Lipstick will last longer if you apply powder to the lips before the lipstick.

3. Use Vitamin E oil or vaseline as an inexpensive alternative to lip gloss.

4. Brush teeth with baking soda to naturally whiten your teeth.

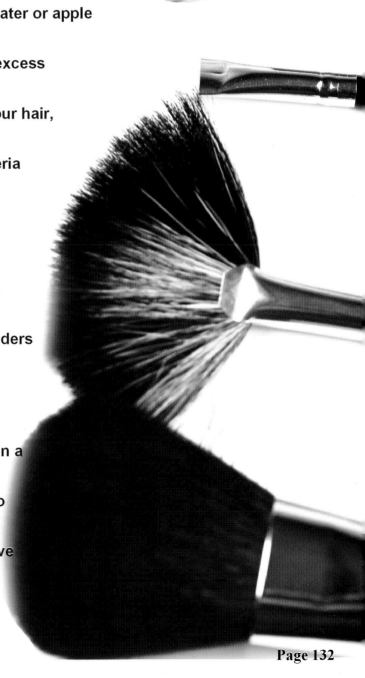

MALE GROOMING

MAN'S GOTTA DO; WHAT A MAN'S GOTTA DO!

th the dawn of the "metro-sexual" era, the spotlight is back on le grooming. Many major companies have launched very ccessful skin care for men over the last few years.

1. When using a hairstyling product, rub it between your palms, then apply to the back of the head first, rather than the front, to prevent gooping or clumping.

2. Try shaving cream or gel, not foam, and use warm, not hot, water on your face. Let the cream sit on your face for a minute or two before shaving, and your shave will be smoother.

3. If you want an at home manicure, simply soak fingertips in warm water with lemon slices . Presoak your nails into the emons, rinse, and dry.

4. If your hair is coarse and frizzy, you probably wash it too much. Just because you are in the shower doesn't mean you need to shampoo. Simply rinse your hair with water or just condition it, and only shampoo every few days.

5. Coffee is a popular body scrub overseas. In the shower, with the help of a washcloth, massage coffee grounds into skin from the neck down to slough off and soften dry, flaky skin.

6. Warm 1 cup of honey in a saucepan. Cleanse and exfoliate your face, then brush a thin layer of warm (not hot) honey onto your face with a small brush or your fingers. Leave on for ten minutes. Rinse.

7. For fast and easy acne treatment, dip a cotton swab in tea tree oil (Found anywhere in any health food store.) Apply oil directly onto blemishes.

8. Wild brows can be tamed by simply combing brows in an upward and use small scissors to cut off any ends that are spiraling wildly out of control.

9. Aloe can be used for a quick tightening mask. Cut the leaf from an aloe plant. Slit it open lengthwise, and rub the exposed gel on your (clean) face. Leave on skin for 10 to 15 minutes, and rinse with cool water.

10. If your hair is brittle, mash an overripe avocado until it looks ready for guacamole. Mix in an egg yolk and two tablespoons of olive oil. Massage it into damp hair, leave in for 15 minutes to an hour. Rinse, shampoo, and condition hair.

THE 5 MINUTE FACE

You won't always have hours to prepare for a casting or shoot. Luckily, it only takes five minutes to create a polished, "pro glam" look. Below are tips and techniques that will help you pull it together in a flash!

STEP 1 SKIN (30 Seconds)

Apply concealer under the eyes and cover any blemishes. Blend well. Then apply foundation or tinted moisturizer. TIP: A powder foundation will cut back on time applying both powder and foundation. It also eliminates shine giving you a polished look.

STEP 2 EYE SHADOW (1 Minute)

Sweep a light, neutral eye shadow all over your lids. Choose a bland shade such as sand, khaki or beige. This will neutralize any red in your lids and bring light to your eyes making them POP. Next, sweep your "statement color" across the crease of your lid with an eye shadow brush. This can be a smokey color for a dramatic look or a natural brown or gray, for daytime wear.

STEP 3 EYE LINER (1 Minute)

Rest your elbows on a table to keep your hands steady. Use a pencil with a soft, not sharp, point and make a swift line as close to the upper and lower lash line as possible. Soften the line by smudging with your finger.

STEP 4 LIPS (30 Seconds)

Color your entire lip with a pencil and top with gloss, or simply slide on lipstick.

STEP 5 CHEEKS (30 Seconds)

Apply a sheer pink or peach blush on the apples of your cheeks and blend well to ensure the edges have no harsh lines.

STEP 5 LASHES (1 Minute)

Curl your lashes and coat them with mascara.

STEP 6 HAIR LIFT (30 Seconds)

Turn your head over and spray some hairspray on your roots. Next, work your hands through hair to give optimum volume.

The art of EYE-CONIC eye shadow

The eyeshadow decides the mood of your entire look. The photos on the right are an example of just a few of the many options you have when choosing your eye shadow. Regardless of the style you choose, the steps to take in applying your eye shadow are the same.

1st: Prep your face with concealer. Pat gently under the eyes to cover any dark circles and hide imperfections.

2nd: Next, groom and define brows with an eyebrow pencil. Fill in the brow using light strokes in the direction of the hair and blend. To really "pop out" eyebrows, brush slightly with mascara.

3rd: Cover the eye with a light, neutral eye shadow. This will neutralize any red in your lids and bring light to your eyes making them POP. Next, sweep your "statement color" across the crease of your lid with an eye shadow brush. Use a smokey color for a dramatic look or a natural brown or grey for daytime wear.

4th: Use a pencil with a soft, not sharp, point and make a swift line as close to the upper and lower lash line as possible. Soften the line by smudging with your finger, or use a small brush.

5th: "Diamonds may be a girl's best friend," but, MASCARA is a model's best friend. No other one item of makeup pops out a woman's face more than lengthening and thickening the eyelashes. Curl and coat your lashes with your favorite mascara. Wait 30 seconds to a minute and apply another coat for added volume.

Choose the right shade for your eye color:

BROWN EYES: Shades of green, bronze, copper, amber, pale blue, and gold will create subtle drama that will deepen the color of your eyes

BLUE OR GRAY EYES: Shades with hints of gray, purple, yellow-gold, or copper bring out the blue or smokey gray

HAZEL OR GREEN EYES: Mauve, gold, lilac, bronze, light brown, khaki will make those gold and green lights flicker.

color

Just liner

metalic

neutral

smokey

THE MAKE-UP
BLOOPER CHECKLIST

Every model has stories of
their most embarrassing
make-up bloopers.
We've made you a
little checklist to
help you avoid
those little
beauty blunders,
as much as
possible .

- [ ] Is there lipstick on your teeth?
- [ ] Are your eyebrows disheveled or wild as weeds?
- [ ] Is your foundation blending with your skin or does it look like a mask?
- [ ] Is your foundation blended above your lips, by the sides of your nose, and in front of your ears?
- [ ] Is there a rigid line of foundation at your jaw line?
- [ ] Is there foundation or powder on your eyebrows or hairline?
- [ ] Are there lines of concealer in the creases of your eyelids or Under your eye?
- [ ] Does your blush look like spots or stripes on your cheeks?
- [ ] Is your lipstick bleeding?
- [ ] Check hair for stray hairs or fly aways.
- [ ] Is there sleep goop in the corners of your eyes?
- [ ] Do a quick breath check before any casting or audition.
- [ ] Are there deodorant marks on the pits of your shirt or clumps under your arms?
- [ ] Is your mascara smudgy?
- [ ] Check for oil or perspiration that makes your face appear "greasy." Keep a compact handy.

"If you are distressed by anything external... the **pain** is not due to the thing itself, but to your **your** estimate of it. Remember, you have the power to revoke it at any time."
-Roman Emperor Marcus

TOP BEAUTY FAQs

Why do diets not work?

Temporary diets do not work because they are temporary. A great diet is a consistent healthy way of eating, and nota 2 week temporary diet. A healthy diet should never make you feel deprived or desperate. Any diet that lasts for a temporary period and makes you starve half to death is a form of self abuse. Quit dieting forever and learn how to eat right from now on. A temporary drastic change in eating habits should be for detoxing the body and not for weight loss. Stop punishing yourself by dieting and start rewarding yourself by eating right. Fad diets tend to focus more on what you eat and not when you eat, which is just as important. You should stop eating at least 3 hours before bedtime.

How do I remove make-up from clothes?

Don't rub make-up stains off of your clothes, as it will only get worse. First soak club soda into the stain. Sprinkle one teaspoon of salt on top to soak up the access liquid, then brush off.

How do I get rid of cellulite?

Cellulite is your body's way of storing toxins in your fat cells. The only way to rid your body of unsightly dimples is to first rid your body of that toxic waste. Once the body flushes out the toxins, then it will naturally flush out the fat cells along with the ugly cellulite. Drink at least four to six glasses of water per day.

What is the best look for me?

Most of us are not celebrities who can afford a personal image consultant and personal stylist. It's best to look at fashion magazines for the latest trends. It is important, however, to stay true to your ethnic look.

1. Asians with blond hair do not look natural.
2. African Americans are not believable with blue contacts.
3. Caucasians with spray tans look like they are from the Jersey Shore.

"This above all else... to thine own self be true"

-Shakespeare

DO WHAT YOU ♥ LOVE

LOVE WHAT YOU DO ♥

WORD SEARCH

Here are words that describe WHO I AM AS A MODEL. Meditate on each quality as you look for it. Words can be vertical, horizontal, diagonal, forward or backward. HAVE FUN!

```
X B L L D T N E D I F N O C F H
L E X P R E S S I V E C A E J A
R A I V E P A T H E A L T H Y N
O U D E A L O S B R Y K T I S D
E T D F M Y T S L S S M A R T S
L I N A E O S F I A U O L D Y O
B F E A R L E S S T E V E C L M
M U N L I I N Z A I I A N W I E
U L G G T Z N X R L W V T N S G
H M S T R O N G L E C Y E Z H H
F A S H I O N A B L E Z D S P L
N G L F A T S P A T I E N C E Q
```

Look for the following words in the "WORD SEARCH " above.

STYLISH	POSITIVE	FASHIONABLE	HEALTHY
EXPRESSIVE	FEARLESS	HANDSOME	TALENTED
VERSATILE	SMART	HUMBLE	STRONG
DREAMER	BEAUTIFUL	CLASSY	CONFIDENT

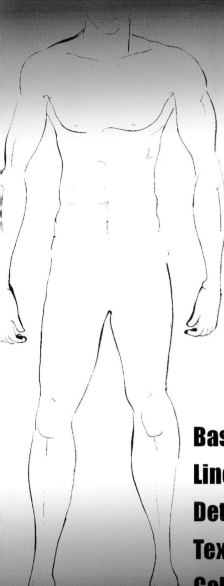

DRAW YOUR OWN HIGH FASHION DESIGN

Basic Principles Of Fashion Design

Line......... Flair, straight, V Neck, Collar

Detail...... Scarf, Belt, Pockets, Buttons

Texture.. Silk, Denim, Khaki, Polyester

Color....... Bold, Pastel, Paisley, Stripped

Hint: If this exercise doesn't look like fun to you, chances are, this is not the area of the industry you are meant to pursue.

BE A FASHION DESIGNER

DO YOU HAVE A
MODEL'S
PERSONALITY?

Take the test below to see if you have the typical professional model's personality.

I WATCH WHAT I EAT.	YES NO
I PRACTICE MY FACIAL EXPRESSIONS IN THE MIRROR .	YES NO
I ENJOY READING FASHION MAGAZINES.	YES NO
I TRY TO WEAR THE LATEST STYLES AND TRENDS .	YES NO
I LOVE TO BE IN THE SPOTLIGHT.	YES NO
I EXERCISE AND WORKOUT ON A REGULAR BASIS.	YES NO
I DON'T TAKE REJECTION PERSONALLY.	YES NO
I GO TO THE MOVIES AT LEAST ONCE A MONTH.	YES NO
I PRACTICE MY CATWALK DOWN MY HALLWAYS.	YES NO
I SING IN THE SHOWER AND DANCE IN THE RAIN.	YES NO
I KEEP MY HAIR/NAILS GROOMED MOST OF THE TIME .	YES NO

If you circled more than 3 NOs... Modeling might not be for you.

SELF IMAGE TEST

This test is to help you evaluate your strengths and weaknesses. You must be completely honest to benefit from the results. Put a "1" by each attribute that applies to you. Deduct the total score on the right from the total score on the left.

I AM +

SELF CONFIDENT ____
CHARISMATIC ____
PHOTOGENIC ____
FIT & FIRM ____
CHARMING ____
PASSIONATE ____
ENTHUSIASTIC ____
SELF MOTIVATED ____
CREATIVE ____
ENERGETIC ____
JUST THE RIGHT SIZE ____
UNFORGETTABLE ____
INTERESTING ____
ENTERTAINING ____
OPTIMISTIC ____
QUIRKY ____
UNIQUE ____
VALUABLE ____
TALENTED ____
BEAUTIFUL ____
TOTAL + POINTS ____

I AM –

SHY ____
TIMID ____
STRESSED ____
SELF CONSCIOUS ____
BORING ____
OVERWEIGHT ____
DEPRESSED ____
PESSIMISTIC ____
MISERABLE ____
NOT POPULAR ____
LAZY ____
PLAIN JANE ____
AVERAGE JOE ____
HOPELESS ____
BLAND ____
UNFULFILLED ____
NOT TALENTED ____
GENERIC ____
APATHETIC ____
NOT COOL ____

MINUS TOTAL - POINTS ____

TOTAL SCORE ____

If you scored +16 or above: you have a healthy self image

If you scored +4 and below: your self image needs to improve

If you scored -5 to +15: you have average self image

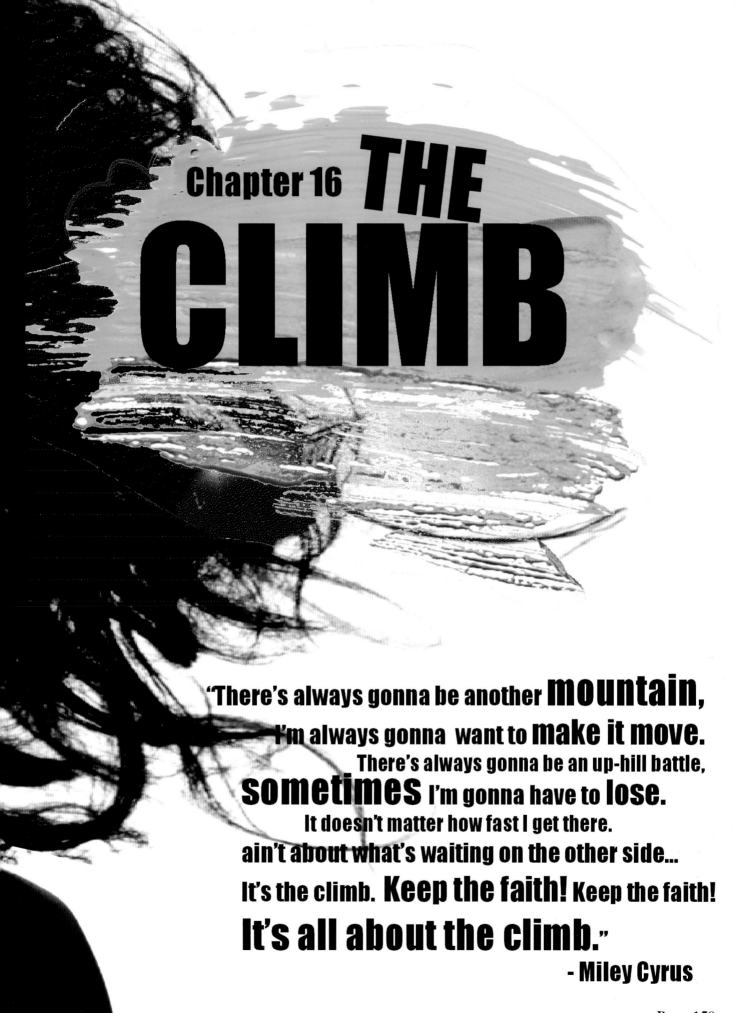

Chapter 16 THE CLIMB

"There's always gonna be another **mountain**, I'm always gonna want to **make it move**. There's always gonna be an up-hill battle, **sometimes** I'm gonna have to **lose**. It doesn't matter how fast I get there. ain't about what's waiting on the other side... It's the climb. **Keep the faith!** Keep the faith! **It's all about the climb."**

\- Miley Cyrus

A CHALLENGE
Leaders see obstacles...

I believe that a challenge is neither positive or negative. Your reaction to the challenge is the determining factor. A challenge is a good thing. Alexander Graham Bell's wife had a challenge of being hard of hearing. This motivated him to create a hearing device, which evolved into the telephone. According to history books, during the same time frame, dozens of other inventors were working on communication devices but did not succeed. Many came close to a worthy hearing machine, but ultimately all failed, quit trying, or gave up. Only Bell had the motivation to keep going. Just like the Energizer Bunny, he kept going and going, never stopping. Why? His motivation was to help his wife! When obstacles hinder you and when problems overwhelm you, there has to be a deeper motivation that inspires you. Like weights on either end of a balancing scale, any challenge that I have faced, no matter how difficult or heavy, has never tipped the scale against my motivation to lead my family.

My strong will and stubborn determination out weighs any failure that comes against me. I get knocked down, but I get up again. I fail miserably, but I try again. The harder the problem, the deeper you have to dig to find the inspiration to face it. Remember, the greatest treasures on Earth, like oil and gold, are hidden deep beneath the surface. Likewise, most people have untapped resources and gifts that are lying dormant deep within themselves. Your attitude will be your rocket fuel to lift you above circumstnces. Bad attitudes create Grinch's and Grinch's steal more than just the joy of christmas. A Grinch sees a glass half empty instead of half full.

"My uncle Sammy was an angry man. On his tombstone it said: "What are you looking at?" - Mararet Smith

Have you ever been to Disney World and watched a family quarrel and fight while trying to have fun? Have you ever watched golfers on a golf course curse at and throw their clubs while trying to have fun? Do you live with a Grinch? Are you a closet Grinch? Are you nice and friendly outside your home, but like Dr. Jeckell and Mr. Hyde, turn into a monster behind closed doors? Unfortunately, anger pours poison toxins into the bloodstream. Bitterness has been scientifically proven to suppress the immune system. In 1920, Clarence Saunders was fired as a young grocery store clerk because he could not retrieve the customers orders fast enough. Instead

Think of your biggest failure to date. Did you learn from it or repeat the same failure again? Keep a journal of your future successes and failures... then study them so you don't miss out on another great learning experience, disguised as a failure.

IS A GIFT
as opportunities.

of being angry at his boss or feeling sorry for himself, he faced his challenge of unemployment and created a self-help grocery store, where the customers could retrieve their own groceries for themselves. This new concept was instantly successful, and Piggly Wiggly became the first national grocery store chain.

Negative people tend to create negative situations. Positive people turn around negative situations. Even the Grinch grew a heart when he learned to give instead of take. His life was transformed when he finally gave up a negative personality.

"Failure is only the end, IF YOU QUIT"
-JIM CARREY

FAILURE:

Failure is like a glass of water... you can see it half empty or half full.

I believe every failure is a blessing in disguise. I fail at something every day. As humiliating as it is, I do not regard failure as a negative thing. I believe failure is nature's way of exposing weaknesses in your goal or plan, and thereby allowing you to make crucial course adjustments. Failure allows you to learn a vital life lesson, that will ultimately make you stronger and more successful. Unfortunately, most people view failure as a good enough reason to quit!!! They then hurry off to a new adventure, which entertains them until they again meet face to face with another failure. Thus, the never ending circle of chasing success without ever realizing that failure is a vital part of the process and crucial to the attainment of your ultimate goal.

A baseball player learns to hit a home run by striking out a thousand times. A musician learns to play on key by missing the note many times. The saying "*practice makes perfect*" is another way of saying, you have to fail many times before you succeed. Successful people are individuals who have the discipline to keep trying, not give up, and never ever quit.

My own personal shyness as a child caused me to never raise my hand during class at school, even when I knew the answer. That weakness escalated during my teen years to abnormal stage fright, which paralyzed my personality. After years of avoiding any type of spotlight or attention to myself, I finally overcame my fear of public speaking and performance and actually entered the "spotlight industry." Thus, my passion for my business!! My greatest weakness to speak in public, became my greatest strength, only because I didn't give up. My fear of rejection has developed into a strong personality of steel. Everyday I still face criticism, but it no longer terrifies me. It actually now strengthens my character. I still fall on my face in front of others, which used to horrify me, but now it no longer bothers me at all.

There was an old miner who had dug for copper for 20 years. One day his beloved mule stepped in a gopher hole and broke his leg. The miner realized that his long time partner must be shot and put down. Instead of giving in to discouragement, despair and depression, the old man

Blessing or Curse?

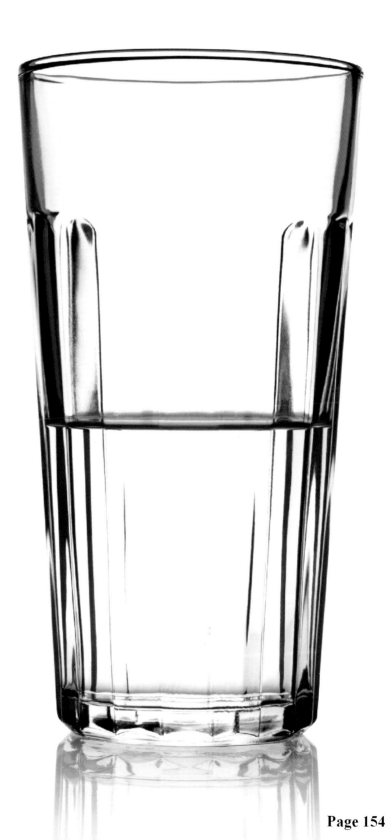

sang as he remembered the years of their ups and downs together as a team. As he dug the grave for his faithful mule, the miner struck the largest vein of copper that he had ever discovered; thus, escalating him to much wealth. Sometimes your greatest success lies just beyond your greatest failures.

"Far better it is to dare to do mighty things... to win **glorious triumphs** and to learn from **devastating failures...** than to rank with those poor spirits who neither enjoy nor suffer much, because they live in the gray twilight that **knows neither victory nor defeat.**"
-Theodore Roosevelt

"Greatness lives on the edge of destruction."

- Will Smith

Live with PASSION

Let's begin. Passionate people are successful people. So rightly define passion. What is passion? It means "enthusiasm for what you are doing." In the Greek, "*En*" means *in...* "*theo*" means *God or divinity*. Therefore, enthusiasm conveys the notion of being *one* with a higher source. Another word that is similar is *inspiration* or "*in*" the "*spirit*." To be inspired or to be enthusiastic about what you are doing, is to be directly ordained to *flow*. On the other hand, passion does not necessarily mean happiness. Take for instance, a marathon runner who is going up a hill at mile 14! His passion, his enthusiasm, and his inspiration have to override his perspiration and lack of happiness at that moment. Happiness comes and goes.

"Being **happy** is something you have to **learn how to do.**"
- Harrison Ford

To have continual passion is to possess a very deep and wide foundation of a bedrock of joy for "who I am" and "what I am doing." Similar to the ocean, the surface may be calm one day and stormy and turbulent the next day, however, deep down underneath the surface, the water is always still... always calm... completely unaffected by the wind or storm that is rocking its surface.

Once you have found your joy in what you are doing, the joy that is deep within your very soul, that is located at the center of your being; you will have then found your anchor that holds your life in tow. Just like the eye of a hurricane, there is an absolute stillness, peace, and calm in the midst of the storm. So how does all of this apply to finding fulfillment as a model? The fulfillment of feelings can only come from the source of feelings... yourself. The job can never satisfy you. Money will never fulfill your deepest needs. People will always disappoint you. Anyone can hurt you, if you give them the power to do so. The power belongs to you, unless you give it away to some someone else. I love my job, but it is not my source of happiness. My kids make me happy some days, but also drive me crazy on other days. Friends come and go. Success only comes from inside of us. When you believe in who you are and what you are doing, you can be successful in the midst of any storm. Keep your eye on your goal. Don't get distracted by challenges or intimidated by obstacles. Learn your craft. Believe in yourself. Don't give up. MAKE IT HAPPEN!

"Because of **Reality TV,** everyone thinks they can be a fashion designer or a model. That is **NOT** the way things go. **LEARN YOUR CRAFT.**"
- Anne Wintour (Editor of Vogue)

Do you really believe in yourself? Do you really believe that you have a goal to reach, that is worth your passion? Then get ready for a challenge. Prepare yourself to conquer and take dominion. Many are called, but few are chosen. The masses of people prefer to sit in the audience and cheer from the sidelines. At a football game, 50,000 people WATCH as about 50 people PLAY. Leaders understand that you have good days & not so good days. There is a fine line between winning and losing. Greatness is on the edge of destruction. Real champions get knocked down, but they know how to get back up. Quitters never win. The grass is not always greener on the other side. Learn to play the game of life right where you are NOW, with the people next to you NOW, doing what you are doing NOW. Quit looking for success around the next corner, and find it right where you are NOW.

Nothing has any value whatsoever, within itself. The value is in the eye of the beholder.

Example #1
Bill's old baseball bat is 34" long, made of wood and is worth about $10 on EBay. Another identical baseball bat is worth $100,000.00 on EBay. Why? Because it belonged to Babe Ruth! Same type bat... different value.

Example #2
Bill's old handkerchief that used to wipe sweat is worth nothing on EBay. A similar handkerchief wiped Elvis' brow and sold for over $200,000.00 on Ebay.

So what's the point? The bats and the handkerchiefs were nearly the same. The only difference is their perceived value.

There was a tribe of people who murmured and complained about how stony their soil was, because it made it bad for farming. They fumed and fretted every year trying to make crops grow on their terrible land. After years of anger and depression, the tribe's leaders decided to pull up stakes and move the tribe hundreds of miles away. Afterward, another tribe moved into the area and also encountered the rocky soil. Instead of complaining, they decided to take up sheep farming instead. The soil was able to produce grassy pastures good enough for sheep grazing. They learned to be prosperous on the land in spite of the rocks. A young shepherd boy from the tribe, put one of the stones from the soil in his pocket. One day, he was hitting the stone with a stick at a nearby trading post, when a man noticed that this boy's shiny stone was actually a diamond. The rocky soil was actually dirt filled with diamonds! The area today is the Kimberly Mines in South Africa, the richest plot of land on the face of the Earth. What was a curse to one tribe became a blessing to the next tribe!

Our crazy little business is surrounded with rocky soil. So what? A rose has thorns. Enjoy the roses. Enjoy your business. Enjoy life! Life is good!

"For every one of my successful inventions, I have one thousand failures."

-Thomas Edison

"My parents' divorce and hard times at school combined to mold me. It gave me the drive to pursue my dreams."

- Christina Aguilera

The SECRET TO SUCCESS

My secret to success is I spend more time counting my blessings than counting my problems. I focus on what I have rather than on what I don't have. Have you ever done something for someone and found that they were extremely grateful in return? It automatically makes you want to do even more for them. On the other hand, when you genuinely give something to someone who doesn't seem to notice or care.... and doesn't demonstrate gratefulness, you will probably not be motivated to continue to give. The universe works under this same principle. Those who are grateful for what they have, seem to get more and more. Where as, those who murmur and complain about what they don't have, seem to continue to spiral downward. Ungratefulness is the root of bitterness, jealousy, envy, and depression. So how grateful to the universe are you?

The next time you eat a salad, try thinking about the farmer who planted and harvested the greens, the trucker who transported them, the cook who prepared the salad, and the waiter who carried it to your table. Don't forget to thank God, who made the rain and the sunshine which created it. Try it next time you eat and I promise you that salad will taste amazing. Be grateful for your food as a beginning, continue being grateful for your health, your family, your job, and watch your energy level rise. Then watch your health and relationships sky rocket. Plant gratitude and harvest prosperity. Show an attitude of gratefulness and reap the rewards of joy and contentment. Show acts of gratitude to your bookers and watch them blossom and shine. Ignore them and take them for granted, and you will be disappointed with their results.

"Gratitude is a vaccine... an antitoxin... & an antiseptic."

-John Henry

FIND SOMETHING OR SOMEONE TO BE GRATEFUL FOR TODAY!

By now you should know exactly

WHERE YOU ARE.

You should have also determined the direction of

WHERE YOU ARE GOING.

After finishing this book, it doesn't matter if you have decided, "yes, **I am** a model" or "no, **I am** not a model." The point is that you now know who you are and what you want to do. Whatever it is that you decide to do, remember that life itself is a climb in an upward direction to a higher position. I guarantee there will be hard work, set backs, highs, lows, good days and bad days.

The bad days should never be taken as a negative factor. To be successful, they have to be viewed as a challenge to produce a positive element. In other words, take life's lemons and make your own lemonade. Find the silver lining behind any cloud. Remember, the antidote to a poisonous snake bite is contained within the poisonous venom itself. The answer to your problem is contained in your problem itself. For example, several publishing companies turned down J.K. Rowlings and her Harry Potter books. She didn't give up, she persevered and became the first author to become a billionaire. Bloomingdale's originally said no to a young unknown designer with wide ties, but eventually changed their mind allowing Ralph Lauren to sell his first fashion item in their store. Decades later, his brand name is one of the most prestigious labels in the world. Sylvester Stallone's script, Rocky was rejected dozens of times. He hung in there just like his fictitious character, and he became a champion at making blockbuster movies.

And finally, everyone knows that Michael Jordan was cut from his high school basketball team! All of these people have one thing in common... They did not see failure as an obstacle. They saw it as an opportunity to pull success from within.

Every model hears the word

"NO" many times.
Rejection is a part of the process.

"Yes" is just around the corner. Don't stop. Believe in who you are. Believe in your dream. As long as you are still breathing, your dream is still alive. No one can take it away from you except yourself. You lose it when you quit. It stops when you stop. Swallow the antidote! That's right. Drink all that poisonous rejection!

Decide to be
better today
than you were yesterday.

Learn from your mistakes! Don't be afraid of obstacles in your path. When the Jews faced the mighty waters of the Red Sea, they had to face the waves and walk directly into their fear. Only when they were neck deep and going under did the waters part before them. Don't turn back, don't go back to Egypt and be a couch potato. Don't be a slave to Pharaoh or the fear of failure that can shackle your mind like chains.

Make up your mind to be more determined than ever. Create a scrapbook or vision board of cutouts from magazines to remind you of your dreams everyday. Keep a journal of your progress. Document the highs and lows. Keep records of weight lost goals and exercise charts. Start BEING a model now. Be creative with your wardrobe today. Try adding unusual accessories. While dressing in your room, model in front of the mirror. While walking down the hall at school, hold your shoulders back and practice walking with perfect posture and poise. Feel the feeling!! Everywhere you go, look for opportunities. Maybe you will begin with landing a small part in your school play. Maybe someone will ask you to join the church choir. Maybe you will see a a sign to audition for a community theatre production. Who knows what will happen? This is your life. You have one shot, so get ready. If you are reading this book, you have already taken the first step. Now its your turn to show off and to

SHINE!
Become a star
right where you are.
Right now!

A MODEL'S DICTIONARY

Everyone's choice of occupation or career usually defines deep down inside of them, who they really are. For example, a nurse is compassionate, a soldier has to be courageous, and an astronaut is usually daring and adventurous. So who is a model? Well, they certainly come in all shapes and sizes! Young models advertise jeans, and older models advertise Metamucil. How do you know if you should pursue a career in the entertainment industry? If your current job leaves you empty and unfulfilled, maybe it is time to pursue a career that dares you to dream! A dream motivates you to achieve greatness. A job gives you a paycheck and pays your bills. A *dream* makes you successful and satisfied. A job is boring and monotonous. Modeling is a *DREAM JOB*. While most people work to live, dreamers live to work. Your work develops your talents and skills. Unfortunately, most jobs don't! Your job should pay you in proportion to your production. Most jobs do not!

This book is both shallow and deep. From mascara to karma... From catwalks to faith... this book is me! Both shallow and deep... just like the song, we are all a little bit country, and a little bit rock and roll.

FOR LIFE

I am a little bit of a monk and a little bit of a model. I AM the best of both worlds.

Here are some shallow and deep terms and concepts that will become essential in helping you focus your time and energy. Tell yourself, "*YES I CAN,*" even if someone shouts back at you, "*NO, YOU CANT.*" Meditate on these principles. Even if you take 1 step forward and 2 steps back, still concentrate on these philosophies. Read them over and over. Their full meaning cannot be understood instantly. The following concepts require time to be fully absorbed. This is my dictionary for life.

GOD
The invisible power which creates.

UNIVERSE
The ideas of the mind of God expressed in visible form.

HAPPINESS
Contentment.

LIGHT
The vibration energy that illuminates God's creations.

DARKNESS
The absence of light . Darkness appears as shadows which are illusions with no power.

THOUGHTS
The activity of the mind.

POVERTY
The belief in lack or limited positive thought.

CREATION
Thought becoming form, the outward manifestation of an inward concept.

LOVE
Positive energy... A synonym for God. Love is a lack of judgment, condemnation, and fear.

SIN
A lack of love. A mistake.

HEALTH
The realization of perfect thought which manifests as perfect life.

IMAGINATION
To form a mental picture in your mind of the desire of your heart.

MAN
A creation of God which has the mental ability to think and create.

ABUNDANCE
Unlimited positive thought.

KARMA
The law of cause and effect.

CONSCIOUSNESS
Awareness.

UNCONSCIOUSNESS
A spiritual coma.

LIFE
Consciousness of power and activity.

WISDOM
The ability to be successful and satisfied.

HELL
The atmosphere of negative thinking.
The belief of separation from God.

FAITH
Positive mental activity.

ATTRACTION
The drawing power of thought.

RICHES
Ideas of abundance.

MANIFESTATION
The result of what you think.

FLOW
Action with no strain or struggle.

TRUTH
That which is not an illusion.

SOUL
The inner creative life, that demonstrates that the kingdom of God is within you.

PERSONALITY
The part of man that makes him as unique as a snowflake and original as a fingerprint. No two are alike.

SAINT AND SINNER
Variable degrees of love and a lack of love.

SELF CONTROL
The personality and the soul in agreement and alignment.

HEAVEN
The atmosphere of positive thinking.
The knowledge of union with God.

"Dictionary for life" (continued)

INTELLIGENCE
The ability to make the best choices.

EVIL
Misuse of God's power.

KNOWLEDGE
Knowing the reality that there is only one omnipotent, omnipresent power.

PEACE
The knowledge that you have done your best.

POISE
An inner calm which never fears. Confidence under pressure. Mental balance.

POWER
The result of the union of peace and poise. The certainty that God abides at the center of our being, as perfect health, complete joy, wisdom and goodness... ready to manifest at our bidding.

ILLUSION
Belief in more than one power.

DESIRE
What you seek that is also seeking you.

MONEY
A symbol of the worth of your service to other people.

FEAR
The belief that the cause of the effect is external.

DESTINY
The purpose of your life.

SELF CONFIDENCE
No fear.

CHARACTER
The pathway to your destiny.

ANGER
The leading cause of disease.

JESUS
The *one* who showed me how to love.

HOME
Your school room for life.

FAMILY
Your school mates for life.

CAREER
Your opportunity to serve by using your talents and gifts.

SOUL MATE
Your best friend for life.

DREAM
Divine power unleashed for potential creation.

DEATH
"It is good." "It is finished."
The end of your journey.

MODEL
A leader!!!
Someone who motivates and inspires people to follow them.

I AM A MODEL!

This book is
DEDICATED

To my husband... **MY SOULMATE.**

Bill, you are the love of my life.

To my family... **MY TEAMMATES**

Lisa, Johnny, Doug, Ashley, Lance, Danielle, April and Grace, you are my very best friends.

To my Grandchildren... **MY PLAYMATES**

Mckenzie, Madison, Macy, Rhili, Brooklynn, Summer, and Molly, you are my treasure here on earth.

Special thanks to my daughter April who made this book happen. Your layout and graphic design made my simple words, on a page, come to life. As usual, you are humble and in the background, letting someone else get the credit... BUT NOT THIS TIME! This book is your masterpiece and I am proud to have been part of it. I love you.

I TIP MY HAT TO YOU..

NOT THE END...
THIS IS THE
BEGINNING

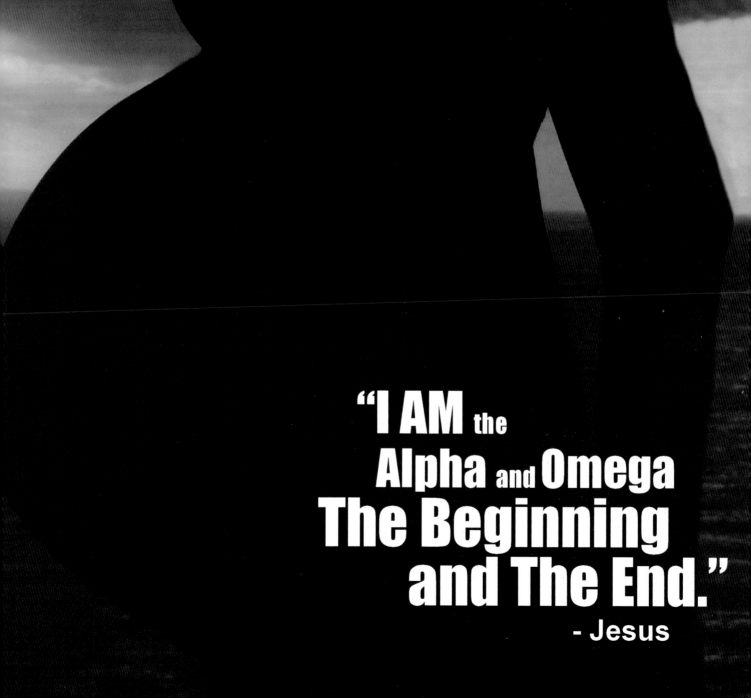

"I AM the
Alpha and Omega
The Beginning
and The End."
- Jesus

Illustrated and Designed By:
April Waldbueser

Published By
MODEL SHOP CO, inc.
475 Brickell Ave, Suite #3215
Miami, FL 33131

WWW.AMMSMODELSHOP.COM

Distributed in Canada By Audition America Model and Talent Search

Distributed in USA By Audition America Model and Talent Search

Printed In The USA

Model Shop IS#: 9er53-23-1256-356-7
          DI#: 268-45-8242-82-33